About

Al Batt of rural Hartland, Minnesota is a writer, speaker, storyteller, and humorist. Al writes four weekly humor and nature columns for many newspapers, and does a show three times per week about nature on a number of radio stations. He is a columnist for *Bird Watcher's Digest* magazine, and he writes a number of popular cartoon strips that are syndicated nationally. He has written for a number of magazines and books, including the *Chicken Soup for the Soul* series. He is a contributing author to the book *Minnesota Bird Watching* and is a trustee of the American Bald Eagle Foundation in Haines, Alaska. He has written for the movies and hosted TV shows for many years. He speaks at various festivals, conferences, and conventions all over the United States and Canada. He has received the Ed Franey Conservation Media Award from the Izaak Walton League, received an award from Bluebirds Across Nebraska for outstanding contributions to wildlife conservation, is a member of *Ray Brown's Talkin' Birds* Hall of Fame, and was given the Thomas Sadler Roberts Award by the Minnesota Ornithologists' Union for outstanding contributions to Minnesota ornithology and birding. Al speaks to anyone who will listen. His mother thinks he is special.

A Life Gone to the Birds

By
Al Batt

Published by:

BIRD WATCHER'S.
DIGEST

Bird Watcher's Digest Press
P.O. Box 110 • Marietta, OH 45750
800.879.2473
birdwatchersdigest.com

Introduction

I have three words for you, "Buy this book."

If you already bought this book, I have three words for you, "Buy another one."

Writing a book is a great experience—one that as a Minnesotan, I am required to add "Uffda!" and "That was different." As an author, I have discovered that it's not that easy to auth.

I started this book when I was eight years old. You'd think it would be thicker. I assure you that there were no brain cells killed during the writing of this book. I know this book will become a cult classic for those who have trouble getting to sleep. Already critics are calling it a book. This will be to literature what lutefisk is to fine dining. If you don't know what lutefisk is, that's OK. Some would say you are among the blessed.

I am reminded of something that happened at our local library. A chicken entered the library and walked up to the desk. The chicken clucked, "Book, book, book, book!"

The librarian set a pile of four books in front of the chicken. The chicken produced a library card, grabbed the books, and went out the front door. I'm not sure how the chicken grabbed them but it did.

An hour later, the same chicken came back into the library. It set the four books down on the desk and said, "Book, book, book, book!"

The librarian wondered what the chicken was doing with the books, but she took the returns and gave the chicken four more books. The chicken hurried out the door.

Another hour passed and the librarian heard a loud "Book, book, book, book!" She looked up from her work and saw the chicken again. The librarian's curiosity had gotten the better of her. She gave the chicken four new books. This time, the librarian followed the chicken a half-mile out of town. The chicken went through a fence and disappeared into a cluster of trees. The librarian climbed over the fence and walked stealthily through the trees until she came to a pond. There, she watched as the chicken gave each book to a frog. As the frog looked at the cover of each book, it said, "Read It. Read It. Read It. Read it."

I tell this story in order to get the word "book" in as many times as possible, because I have always believed that chickens and frogs have a secret kinship, and because it offers a glimpse of what you might expect from this book. I have had a life-long love and concern for nature. Being outdoors brings me wonder and joy. I never clean my office. I want to preserve habitat.

Thank you for not having anything better to do than to read this book. While on the subject of thanking people, I believe that it's impossible to thank people too much. However, it has occurred to me that many of those who deserve a firm thanking probably would prefer that no one knew that they had anything to do with this book. So, I will thank my wife and then thank everyone else—you know who you are. Thank you to my long-suffering wife and lovely bride, Gail. I can't stop there. Thanks to my wonderful parents who excused my idiosyncrasies and allowed me to become a birdhead. Thanks to *BWD*, Bill Thompson, III, Jim Cirigliano, and to all those who wanted to tell me to go fly a kite, but were too nice, so they told me that I should write a book instead. Thanks to all those who have walked a trail with me and in the process, enhanced my existence. Lastly, to that girl in my fifth grade class who sneered at my six-page book (double-spaced on wide ruled notebook paper) about the cowboy who rode a horse named Cow and brought evildoers to justice by giving them disapproving looks. To her I say, "Neener, neener, neener."

—*Al Batt*

This book is dedicated to my beloved wife Gail, to my family, and to whomever taught you how to read.

Contents:

Chapter 1:
My Fledgling Years

The Friendly Skies

I spent my formative years living on a farm nestled alongside a gravel road. People waved or honked when they drove by. Gravel roads are friendly places. I think that Canada geese might be the friendliest birds we have. I've been watching flocks pass overhead. Not a single flock of the friendly fowl neglects to honk and wave.

Those Thrilling Days of Yesteryear

I'd toss a lopsided baseball filled with sawdust into the air. I'd pretend to toss my catcher's mask to the side and the ball nestled into my Rollie Hemsley model catcher's mitt with a satisfying plunk. I was waiting to commit baseball. Kids ran onto the make-do field. The infield positions filled quickly with older boys. Everyone else moved to the outfield. Most of the outfielders were disappointed or angry to be where they were. Few batters could hit the ball to the outfield, so it could be a boring location.

I stood in center field. I pounded my ancient catcher's mitt while listening to the call of a vesper sparrow. It sang, "Here, here, there, there, everybody down the hill."

It was a good day. I listened to a bird and I almost caught a ball. I hoped Rollie Hemsley was proud.

From Out of the Past

When I was a boy, I was told that if I put salt on a bird's tail, I could catch it. I tried. I never could get salt on the tail of any bird other than a chicken. And I had to catch the chicken first in order to salt its tail, so it didn't do much to prove the method worked. Eventually, someone told me that if I could get close enough to put salt on a bird's tail, I wouldn't need the salt. I would be close enough to catch it. It was just another story that parents told kids for some hidden reason like the tale I heard that said that eating the crust of the Wonder Bread would make hair curly. I wasn't that crazy to have curly hair and I ate the crust anyway, but this was a way to get kids to eat something they didn't want to eat. I'd dismissed the salt legend until one day, in a cartoon I saw Sylvester the Cat putting salt on Tweety's tail so that Tweety couldn't fly away. Then I heard the Mamas and the Papas singing, "This little bird, she can fly away; No salt on her tail. No cage to make her stay."

Inspired by the two messages, I captured a pigeon. It was a beautiful gray bird with the look of a racer. I salted the pigeon's tail liberally. I set it free. It flew like the wind. I concluded that salting a bird's tail is something that works only in cartoon and song.

Walking with Dad

As a boy, I would move with my father at a slow amble, through woodlands, prairies, and wetlands. My father would tell me about the birds, plants, mammals, and insects.

I am so grateful to my father for spending that time with me. A German named Von Herder wrote in the 17th century, "The best powers of the human mind remain dormant until they are ignited into flame by a spark from another human being."

The things found on a walk may seem mundane to some, but every living thing has its inherent magnificence. Robert Michael Pyle wrote, "What is the extinction of a condor to a child who has never seen a wren?"

My father taught me that if you guide a child one day, that experience guides that person for the rest of his or her life. Because of my father's guidance, I have had the great joy of leading countless nature walks. They are an investment in the future.

I walked with my father. I walk with others. I'm closing the loop.

The Bird Hall of Fame

To plant a seed and expect it to grow is an example of great faith.

To expect farm equipment to cooperate fully in such an endeavor is just plain foolishness.

I remember being broken down in the field one spring. That spring was a particularly hectic time—even more so than the typical spring. There was plenty of pressure. The chores had been done before we had made our way to the field. The pigs, chickens, and beef cattle had been fed. The Holsteins had been milked. The weather threatened to turn nasty and chase us from our work. My father sniffed the air. He could tell when weather was changing, especially if rain was coming. I sniffed the air, too. All I could tell for sure was that I had sniffed the air. Dad said it was going to rain. We rushed to complete the repairs.

We hurried to beat the weather. Wrenches hid and knuckles bled when the recovered wrenches slipped from nuts. Tempers that had been dormant suddenly flared. It was a day sponsored by Alka-Seltzer.

In the midst of the growling, we paused to listen to the

song of the vesper sparrow—one of my father's favorite birds.

My father, who taught me to love birds, flowers, and trees, and I both found patience in the song of that fine bird.

I immediately put the vesper sparrow into my Avian Hall of Fame. The induction process was a brief one. I wished it so.

I had learned that the song of a bird isn't just nice to hear. It is a part of us. When I hear the song of a vesper sparrow or a western meadowlark, it revives slumbering memories. The birds and their songs are me.

We fixed the problem with our farm implement. The crop was planted. The field produced a good yield. We didn't make more money than we had ever dreamed of, but we were still rich.

We had shared the song of the vesper sparrow.

Skunk Tales

I was driving down the road the other day when I encountered the aroma of a skunk.

The smell of skunk in the air is a sign of spring.

Smells are great producers of memories. Even fetid odors.

Suddenly, I was a small boy crawling on my hands and knees under an old farm wagon following a black and white critter while I called, "Here kitty, kitty, kitty." Apparently, I was a lonely boy, desperate for feline companionship.

I was very young—a free-range farm boy who looked like he was perpetually in the state of being remodeled. The cat that I was pursuing was in reality a skunk. I was so new to the world that the distinction between skunks and cats was still a bit murky in my mind.

The skunk helped me understand the difference.

Far from being the benign creature portrayed by Flower in the movie *Bambi* the polecat Pepe Le Pewed me. It gave me no warning. Not even a, "Put up your dukes." It was a furry stink bomb. It must have been something I said. The skunk's aim was much better than my mammal identification skills.

I crawled out from under the wagon, reeking of skunk and whimpering, "That kitty stinks."

I ran to the farmhouse, seeking immunity from the essence of skunk. I didn't need to explain things to my mother. She quickly sensed what had happened. Eau de polecat.

My mother acted fast. She called family, friends, and neighbors in order to accumulate all of the tomato juice that she could.

Our home entertained visitors bearing tomato juice. My pungent scent occasioned comments from everyone.

I got a long bath in tomato juice. Tomato juice was the recommended curative for dogs that had tangled with skunks. The acidic juice was supposed to neutralize the alkaline odor of the skunk spray. It was believed that the juice would remove the effluvium of skunk from my young body. Neighbors, friends, and family members peeked at me in my tub of crimson. Not only was my body red, so was my face.

Did it work?

Sort of.

My father said that after my bath, I smelled like a skunk that had been taking swimming lessons in Tomato Juice Lake.

What do you do if your dog brings home a gift from Pepe Le Pew? Try a homemade skunk odor eliminator. Mix one quart of three-percent hydrogen peroxide with one-quarter cup of baking soda and 1 teaspoon of liquid soap. Wet the dog. Wash the dog with this concoction, being careful to keep it out of its eyes, nose, and mouth. Work it through its fur and let the mixture soak on the dog for 5 minutes. Thoroughly rinse Fido with water. Wipe the dog with paper towels so you can dispose of them. Discard the remaining mixture.

Some folks dilute vinegar with water, soap the sprayed areas, apply the vinegar, leave it on for a few minutes and then soap again. Be certain not to get any vinegar in the dog's eyes.

I learned a couple of things after my run-in with the skunk. I discovered that a skunk could make a lot of money teaching self-defense classes. And I realized that I would never like tomato juice as much as I should.

The world is full of coincidences. While the skunk smell still entertained my olfactory system as I traversed the rural road, the radio played "Dead Skunk" by Loudon Wainwright III. "Take a whiff on me, that ain't no rose! Roll up yer window and hold your nose. You don't have to look and you don't have to see, 'cause you can feel it in your olfactory."

I was living that song as I steered my Pontiac down the rural highway.

I like skunks, but I wouldn't want to be stranded on a desert island with one.

I pulled off the road and drove to a small town café for breakfast.

I didn't order the tomato juice.

The Crow

How do crows keep from being hit by cars?

I see the large black birds feeding on an opossum that had been unlucky in its road crossing endeavors. Just when I think a Buick is going to hit them, the crows fly into the air, neatly avoiding a collision, and land behind the car before the car's exhaust fumes have cleared the air. They don't miss a bite of the roadkill. How do they do it? It's simple. The crows have a watchcrow on duty at all times. Whenever a car gets close, the watchcrow cries, "Car! Car! Car!" and everyone flaps to safety.

Henry Ward Beecher said, "If men wore feathers and wings, a very few of them would be clever enough to be crows." Crows and ravens are the class valedictorians of the bird school. You do not sneak up on a crow. You will rarely see a crow that doesn't see you first.

My father told me that crows could count to six. In his youth, he participated in crow hunts. If there were six hunters in a grove and the crows spotted them, the crows would not come close until all six of the hunters had walked out of the woods.

There are those who say that Noah should have drowned both crows when he had a chance. Pay these people no mind as they say the same thing about mosquitoes and what would we do for exercise in the summer if we didn't have skeeters to swat? A crow has a number of unflattering things said about it. It is an accused and convicted corn thief. People talk about having "to eat crow," "to crow about something," and to have "crow's feet." The crow has been associated with unsavory characters in folklore, books, and movies. The crow is depicted as the pet of evil sorcerers or practitioners of black magic.

An ice fisherman friend tells me of watching a crow pull a fish line out of the hole in the ice and eat the minnow that was serving as bait.

A group of crows is called a murder. A murder that loves to mob owls. It's a spectator sport to crows. I once felt sorry for the owls, thinking, "Why don't those crows leave that poor owl alone? Don't they know that it works nights? It needs its sleep." Then I realized that owls get their revenge by going into crow colonies at night and turning a crow or two into lunch. So when crows mob owls, it is to mock a killing bird.

Crows adjust easily to most habitats. Once simple country folks, crows have become street-smart city birds. Cities provide food, warmth, and fewer owls—definite advantages for a crow searching for an apartment.

Crows can sometimes be a bit of a problem in a garden.

When I was a boy, my dog Rex and I would chase the crows from our garden so often that both boy and dog would reach the point of exhaustion. Crows could fly much better than we could and they would taunt us from a safe distance. I decided it would save a lot of running if I built a scarecrow to do the chasing for me. I built a nasty-looking scarecrow. It was so scary that I was not without fear while building the thing. It caused me nightmares. I put my new creation in the garden, feeling sorry for what the crows were going to go through. I needn't have worried. Before the scarecrow's first day in the garden was over, the crows were using him as a perch. It was a perfect place for them to sit, preen their feathers, and discuss human stupidity.

As a last ditch attempt to save steps, I put a mirror in the garden. I leaned one of my sister's old mirrors (I needed mine and girls always have an ample supply of mirrors) against my formerly spooky scarecrow. I thought this would confuse the crows right out of the county. The next day, I checked on my clever solution to our crow problem. My sister's mirror had fallen prey to a dastardly deed. It was covered from top to bottom by crow poop. Their aim was very good.

Honey

My father was not a big fan of television.

He thought that most of it—other than pro wrestling

and any program featuring country-western music—was a complete waste of time. He decided that I, the baby of the family, would not be ruined by the evil boob tube.

"Pick one show that you want to watch and you won't have to help with the milking that night," said my father.

Wow. Talk about needing to make a major decision. I found a *TV Guide* and studied it as I had never studied a textbook. After some deliberation, I found the show for me, *The Wonderful World of Disney*. It was a magical show. In the time before PBS, Discovery Channel, and Animal Planet, Disney was the place to see great nature shows. I loved *The Wonderful World of Disney*.

I informed my father of my decision and he approved my night of freedom from the milk cows and barn chores. One night, I was watching Disney when they had an episode about honeybees and beekeepers. To say it was of interest to me would be an understatement. It showed how beekeepers used smoke to get the delicious honey away from the bees. I salivated as I watched this show. My favorite snack at the time was some white bread with some butter, a little white sugar, and heaps of honey on it. Honey and sugar sandwiches were sublime.

After the program ended, I picked up the phone and called my neighbor Crandall. Crandall was a year or two older than I was, but he was in my grade. He told everyone that he had been redshirted, but he was completely inept at every sport he tried. I liked doing things with Crandall. He was a slower runner than I was. That was a good trait in an accomplice. That meant that whatever was chasing us would catch Crandall first.

"Crandall," I said. "Did you watch the *Wonderful World of Disney* tonight?"

"You bet," replied Crandall. "Honey and sugar sandwiches." Crandall was almost the gourmet I was.

"I have an idea," I went on. Most people have someone who is willing to listen to them and to believe in them, regardless as to how harebrained an idea may be. Crandall was my guy. "Meet me at 10 o'clock tomorrow morning," I said, "And bring your Dad's Zippo lighter, the one he got in the Navy."

The next morning came and Crandall showed up at the appointed time.

I had decided not to involve my parents in my scheme. I'd learned that when it came to parents, it was easier to ask forgiveness than to get permission.

"Here's the plan," I said. "Next to the gas barrels by the house is an old maple tree that was hit by lightning. Part of it broke off, leaving a big hole in the trunk. A squirrel nested there for a couple of years, but honeybees have taken over. You ought to hear all of the buzzing in that tree. You know what that means?"

"Honey and sugar sandwiches!"

I got an old ladder I'd made out of cottonwood and leaned it against the maple tree. It was missing a couple of rungs where I'd run out of nails. I had a broken pitchfork handle wrapped in an old gunnysack, which I'd dipped in gasoline. I would go up the ladder first, carrying the pitchfork handle with me. Crandall would follow. He'd light the sack with his father's Zippo lighter and then wave a peach-colored sports section of the *Des Moines Register* that my Grandma Batt had given me. This would blow the smoke down into the bee tree, just like the bellows that beekeepers use. It would stun the bees so that they won't even know what hit them.

Honey and sugar sandwiches danced in my mind as up the old crooked, cottonwood ladder the two of us went.

We were careful to take a big step where the two rungs were missing. The homemade torch was smoking up a storm thanks to the Zippo with an image of a battleship on it. I held the torch over the hive and Crandall whipped the *Des Moines Register*'s sports section through the air at a furious pace. It was working. I was a bit surprised. I had never had a scheme that worked before. The bees were definitely stunned. They didn't know what hit them. I looked back at Crandall. He was drooling. I could almost taste the honey. Then something went horribly wrong. The sack burned across the top of the pitchfork, allowing the rest of the flaming cloth to fall down into the bee tree. The bees went from being stunned to being very angry. Always thinking of others, I thought I should warn Crandall. I turned, but all I could see of Crandall was a speck on the horizon. Crandall had been to school several years longer than I had and he had learned things in those years. He may have learned them accidentally, but he learned them.

He had decided to save himself. The bees came out of the hive just as they do in the TV cartoons. They formed a huge eye staring at me. My thoughts flashed to the need to save myself. I tossed the pitchfork handle and scurried down the ladder. In my haste to get down the ladder, I had forgotten about the missing rungs. Instead of going down the ladder, I went through the ladder. This proved a good thing, as the bees, being intelligent, expected me to go down the ladder rung-by-rung. By going through the ladder, I lost them for an instant. This gave me a slight head start.

Forgetting about honey and sugar sandwiches, I raced towards the safety of our house. I had never run faster in my life. As I ran north, the bees were prodding me on my south end.

I made it to the house and slammed the door on an angry horde of bees.

I don't know how many times I had been stung; it was too much of a challenge for my limited math skills. My father who had been working in the machine shed was unable to get into the house because of the huge swarm of bees circling it. For several hours, the bees flew past the door, buzzing "Send out the boy! Send out the boy!"

I learned a couple of things from this experience. First, store-bought honey is more than good enough for the likes of me. Second, whenever *The Wonderful World of Disney* was on TV, I was in the barn.

The Snipe Hunt

The older boys said that I needed to go snipe hunting with them. Snipe hunting was a rite of passage wherein older adolescents took younger boys into the wilderness for the express purpose of hunting snipe on moonless nights. The older boys believed the snipe to be an imaginary game bird. The victim was given a burlap bag with which to catch the birds, while the connivers had flashlights to locate the snipe. The conspirators made birdcalls, crying out "snipe" to make the target believe that there were snipe in the area. The schemers claimed to have seen a snipe and pretended to venture forth to drive it to the bagman. The dupe was abandoned by the older boys, who told everyone they encountered about the prank. The cycle repeated when the sucker became privy to the joke and hoodwinked others into searching for the ever-elusive snipe. I thought of that proposed hunt when I heard the winnowing sound made by the feathers of a snipe in flight. There really is a snipe. The snipe, a common shorebird of wet grasslands, has an extremely long bill that it uses to probe in the mud for invertebrates. I didn't fall for the prank when I was a boy because I knew that there was a bird such as a snipe and I didn't want to hunt one. The snipe is so difficult to hunt that it brought about the use of the word "sniper" to describe a sharpshooter in the early 19th century.

Peeping

I listen to the aubade.

The birds sing me out of bed. The spring peepers—small frogs in our temporary ponds—peep loudly. Frogs and birds peep the day away.

I miss another peeping. It's the sound of the mail-order chicks that would peep incessantly in the post office.

It was a big day when we got to pick up the baby chickens. We'd place the chicks in a brooder house. We fed them chick starter and they stayed warm under a heat lamp. We guarded them from fox, weasel, mink, raccoon, and owl. We'd watch the chickens grow to adulthood. We'd gripe if we got more roosters than we felt we should have.

Looking back, it was a great time. I loved sitting in that brooder house, talking to those baby chicks.

Each day, I'd give a shout out to my peeps.

Bird Calls

On our vacations, we stayed home and worked.

Except for one day.

My family went on one big trip a year.

We planned this annual excursion for weeks. It was the closest we came to a vacation.

We went to the Minnesota State Fair for a day. Minnesota's Great Get Together, otherwise known as the day that the cows were milked too early—at three in the morning instead of five. The untimely milking made both cows and humans cranky.

My mother packed a lunch in a picnic basket so we wouldn't be dependent upon deep-fried foodstuffs on-a-stick for our nourishment and placed the basket into the trunk of our old Pontiac. My father, more comfortable in a tractor seat than a car seat, drove the 100 miles to the fair. It was all uphill. Upon arrival at the fairgrounds, we poured out of the Pontiac and synchronized watches so we could meet at the family car for a steamy picnic lunch from the sweltering trunk. I couldn't keep a watch running, so my mother provided me with a windable wristwatch that was missing a band. It was a poor man's pocket watch. It took forever to synchronize our watches. The time kept changing as I attempted to set it. I could never find the time to get it right.

Once the timepieces were somewhat synchronized and our lunchtime set, my father headed to Machinery Hill to kick the tires of expensive tractors that he would never drive. He told us that he didn't want to see any of us until it was time to go home and he wasn't seen again until then. My mother visited the 4-H, poultry, cooking, and sewing exhibits.

Before deserting us, my father would give me a dollar and ask me not to tell my mother. "You know how she is with money," he'd say.

My mother would give me a dollar, saying, "Don't tell your father. You know how he is with money. He is tighter than bark on a tree."

I swore to both that my lips were sealed.

I was a free-range child. With the small amount of money that I had managed to save plus the $2 my parents had given me burning a hole in my pocket, I searched for something to waste my hardly-earned cash on.

Each year, a man had a booth from which he sold a miraculous tiny instrument crafted of leather and metal that he used to produce the most wondrous of birdsongs. He placed the device in his mouth and a heavenly choir of angels sang. An unseen sparrow/wren/thrush/warbler feathered barbershop quartet performed my favorites.

He claimed his song was a cross between a winter wren and a water ouzel. He added that I'd likely sound better than he did.

That sounded good to me.

We raised chickens. I spent a lot of time in the company of chickens. I listened to them. I had heard of people who could call in birds by making a sound like birds. I tried that, but I had spent too much time listening to buff Orpingtons, white leghorns, black silkie bantams, Rhode Island reds, Araucanas, silver laced Wyandottes, and blue cochins. I thought of the araucanas (Easter egg layers) as the robins of the henhouse as they produced lovely blue eggs. Cackleberries, I called them, with a cackle of my own. I might have spent too much time in the company of chickens. Every birdcall I attempted sounded just like a chicken. I tried. I really did. I tried calling in a wood thrush and the neighbor's Plymouth rocks flocked to me.

I consoled myself by the knowledge that chickens are still birds. That worked for me until I came across the bird-calling huckster at the fair.

I delighted in birds. Each year, I promised myself that I wouldn't buy another of those magic devices as I already had a drawer full of them. It was a quiet drawer. None of the birdcalls ever produced a sound.

Each year, I'd fall under the spell of this expert pitchman's line and buy another birdcall or two or three. Hope springs eternal. Since there was no guy in a booth showing me how I could fly like a bird, I was determined to sound like a bird. I had difficulty singing like a human, so I figured I was meant to sing like an avian vocalist. I had good tutors. The western meadowlark provided the background music on our farm. I marveled at the songs of the vesper sparrow, indigo bunting, song sparrow, and gray catbird. The flutelike, ethereal stylings of the wood thrush gave me a lump in my throat. I thought the brown thrasher repeated things for my benefit. It thought I wasn't listening. Birdsongs made me see what I would not see otherwise. I had tried to live by a line from Thoreau, "If he has voice, I have ears."

The money disappeared much too quickly at the Minnesota State Fair. So did time. My semi-synchronized watch with the missing band told me it was time to go home.

In what seemed moments after milking the cows early in the morning, I was seated in the aged Pontiac traveling home to a late milking. My mother talked about preserves and my father declared his astonishment over the expanding size of farm equipment. I patted my pocket where the birdcalls were safely ensconced. I had no doubt that they would change my life.

We milked the cows late into the night. The cows and the humans were tired. The process differed only slightly from the morning's chores.

The cows had the pleasure of listening to me fail to produce birdcalls for yet another year. My enthusiasm was unable to overwhelm the silence. All that the cows heard was my mumbled grumbling.

This occurrence was repeated year after year and involved generations of cows. I tormented the dairy cattle with the wheezing of birdcalls gone bad. Instead of the warble of wren or ouzel, I sounded like the Big Bad Wolf with asthma. No quitter, I continued to practice in a barn of bovine critics.

That is the reason why few cows are ardent birders.

Cardinal Christmas

I grew up on a dairy farm in Minnesota.

That is, what little growing up I've done.

My ancestral home was a marsh thinly disguised as a farm. The farm included Mule Lake—which was more of a swamp than a lake, the Le Sueur River that ran through the farm, and a substantial number of acres that were in a woods consisting entirely of deciduous trees—not a single conifer in the bunch.

The nearest town of any size was Hartland. I'm not sure what constitutes a "town of any size," but Hartland had a population of around 300.

Because our farm had nary an evergreen tree and Hartland sold no Christmas trees, we made a yearly pilgrimage to a tree lot in a city even larger than Hartland. The lots were typically run by a service club, a church organization, or a youth group.

One year, the world conspired against my family acquiring a Christmas tree. One catastrophe after another hit. There were water problems in both the house and the barn, a cow required the services of a veterinarian, and the Pontiac wouldn't start. It was never a surprise when the car didn't start. It had an engine block when it came to starting—it was a mechanical writer's block. It would start only when threatened with jumper cables.

We didn't get to the tree lot much before Christmas. We pulled the Pontiac into the first lot we saw. It had only one tree left.

"Let's go somewhere else," I whined

"No, this is perfect," my father said. "There's no decision required here. Someday you'll appreciate not having to make decisions."

My father was always saying things that made no sense until I became the age he was when he said them.

Dad picked up the pitiful pine. Most of its remaining needles took the opportunity to jump to the ground.

"Ain't she a beauty," said the pine broker with the appearance of a Dickens character.

"No, she isn't," said Dad. "Is this a tree?"

"What do you want for only $5?" said the man.

"I'll give you $3 for it." My father was frugal. We were so poor that we didn't have diamonds in our deck of cards because they were too expensive.

"Sold."

Dad grimaced a little, thinking he should have offered $2, but a deal was a deal.

What a miserable tree it was. There wasn't a bough capable of holding an ornament.

"It's Christmas," my mother said. "We'll learn to love the tree. We'll throw some tinsel on it. I'll use the kind that the dog won't eat. I remember that present she left under the tree for us last year."

We found room on the tree for a few ornaments by measuring the placement of the decorations in order to keep the tree from tipping over.

"I don't think the cat will tip this one over. He likes a challenge," said Dad.

It was a Christmas tradition at our house for the old tomcat to crawl into the tree and send it crashing to the floor between the hours of two and three in the morning. This calamity brought forth a barrage of barks from the canine section of our pet kingdom.

I looked at the meager tree and realized that it wouldn't

offer much room for presents. It hadn't been a profitable year—even by our less-than-lofty standards.

My favorite ornament was a snowflake that had been broken many times and glued back together as best as it could have been. There was no other snowflake identical to that one. While finding the perfect spot to position the snowflake, I saw it—a red feather jammed into the tree near its top. A feather that was once the property of a redbird—a cardinal. Our cardinals came only on Christmas cards. We had no redbirds on our farm in those thrilling days of yesteryear. I know because I looked for them.

The family gathered and wondered how the feather had found itself in its current location. Was it put there by human hand or molted by the bird in the fall? We tried not to think of the bird falling to a predator. However it had arrived, it was part of our Christmas tree.

We placed a shining star at the top of the tree. The feather pointed to it.

A magical thing happened. The imperfections of the tree vanished. Suddenly, it was the most beautiful tree I had ever seen. The feather had turned a forlorn tree into a masterpiece.

I don't remember what I got for Christmas that year, but I remember that feather.

A bird can change the direction of a day and so can a beautiful feather.

I know because I had a cardinal Christmas.

The Hen was in Shock

Chickens were an important part of my family's history. Chickens and their eggs helped us endure. We'd obtained an interesting mixture of species from Murray McMurray Hatchery. One day I heard squawking, and I ventured forth to investigate. I saw a hawk mantling one of the pullets. When a hawk mantles, it spreads its wings, fans its tail, and arches over a prey item, in an action meant to hide it from other predators.

I hollered and ran towards the hawk. The raptor waited until I was close before it took flight. The chicken was motionless. I couldn't tell if it was severely injured. Suddenly, the chicken ran into the henhouse. The hen was OK other than a few missing feathers and maybe some recurrent nightmares.

The Pheasant that Wouldn't Leave

The snow globe had lost its fascination.

I looked outside at a world of cold and snow and more snow.

A single hen pheasant walked to my feeding station. She was brave and hungry. Maybe "desperate" would be a better description, because she came close to humans. Pheasants don't like people. People shoot them. It's hard to like someone who shoots you. The winter can be hard on us all. The bird needed food. I hoped the corn that I had put out would say, "Come on in, the weather is fine."

We mowed a lot of hay on the farm when I was a whippersnapper. We had cows to feed and they ordered hay. I looked hard for nesting birds while I mowed the alfalfa. Pheasants and mallards were common nesters in the hay ground. One day, I hit a nesting hen with the mower. The mower's sharp sickles killed the hen quickly but spared the eggs. I felt terrible. I jumped from the tractor and grabbed the eggs hurriedly, emptying my lunch bucket to find room for the pheasant fruit, and ran to our building site. I made haste to the henhouse. There I located a bantam hen hunkered down in a nest. This banty hen was known for her urge to incubate. She would attempt to hatch golf balls, tennis balls, and any kind of egg. Banties are the pitbulls of the poultry world. When I tried to gather an egg from under a banty hen, she'd peck me. It was a mean-spirited act intended to cause me to find eggs elsewhere.

I placed the orphaned pheasant eggs under the hen. The banty hen was good at her job and took the task seriously. She could focus. She hatched all the pheasant eggs and raised the chicks as her own. The young pheasants became teenagers, at least in behavior, before chickens would have. The chicks prospered but never warmed to people. They didn't fly crazily around the henhouse at my appearance, but they remained wild birds. One by one, they wandered away from the friendly confines of our henhouse and returned to the wild. I hoped they would remember the little hen on Mother's Day. The number of pheasants hanging out with the chickens was soon reduced to one—a rooster that refused to leave. He was like a drummer living in his parents' basement. I named him Phil.

Phil was a fighter. The banty roosters were renowned for their strutting and for their fighting ability. They would get up with the chickens and immediately look for a fight. The banty roosters found a fight in Phil. He was good. Phil used some sort of ancient Chinese pheasant martial arts practiced by only a select few. He took on all comers and defeated them all. The trouble with banty roosters is that they don't know when they are licked. They kept coming back for more. The fights escalated to the point where the pheasant killed several of the banties.

Phil crowed a victorious cow-cat after each encounter.

"That pheasant has to go," said my father. He looked at me and added, "I drew straws and you got the short one. Do something."

My father was a dedicated carnivore. I could see a cartoon bubble over his head featuring a cooked Phil on the dinner table.

I couldn't let that happen. I didn't want to do Phil any harm. I was the one who put Phil into his predicament. He wasn't cuddly or appreciative, but I liked Phil.

I took a cue from the banty hen and hatched a plan.

My alarm went off long before the dark of the night had begun to fade. I grabbed a gunnysack and made my way into a henhouse featuring so many cracks that all the light had been let out. It was a place where it was easier to trip in the darkness than to trip the light fantastic. I employed a flashlight offering a flicker of light. Our flashlights were nothing more than storage units for dead batteries.

I located Phil. He was perched on the section of the roost that was considered prime real estate to fowl. I shined the light into Phil's eyes. I grabbed his feet and moaned a bit at the sharpness of a spur. I apologized as I stuffed a struggling Phil into the gunnysack.

I placed Phil into my old Ford and hauled the kidnapped rooster pheasant many miles away. I waited until daybreak to release Phil because I did not want him to have to find his way in the dark.

I thought about Phil as I watched the hen pheasant swallow corn as quickly as possible at my feeder. I feel a bit guilty about the kidnapping.

I feed the pheasants every winter.

I do it for Phil.

Whom are You Calling a Turkey?

I once got a turkey in bowling.

It wasn't my fault. The bird had no business being in a bowling alley.

I have been called a turkey many times. It's a compliment.

Ben Franklin was a fan of the wild turkey. Ben said that the turkey would have been a better choice for our national bird than the bald eagle.

I never knew Ben, but he seemed like an interesting fellow. He used to take air baths. That's interesting. I don't know about the turkey being our national bird. I can't picture a young man celebrating the accomplishment of becoming a Turkey Scout, or fans cheering as the Philadelphia Turkeys scored a game-winning touchdown. It would be difficult to soar like a turkey when surrounded by eagles.

Turkeys begin as eggs—usually turkey eggs. They hatch into poults. The young males are called jakes and the young females are called jennies. The adult females are hens and the adult males are called toms. I took up turkey calling once, but I foolishly purchased a cheap caller that would only call them Dick or Harry. They did not respond.

Some folks in my neck of the woods raised and released wild turkeys. The big birds like to roost in trees. They tried perching on my neighbor Still Bill's TV antenna. Still Bill—he makes more dust than miles—became exercised when his antenna suffered a severe turkey bend. It didn't help the TV reception or the reception the turkeys received when visiting Still Bill's yard.

A pastor asked me what he could do to get rid of a flock of turkeys that had been roosting regularly on the roof of the church. I drove to the church and saw the congregation of turkeys. I advised the minister that he should immediately baptize and confirm the flock. If he did that, he would see them only at Christmas.

When I was a mere sapling before growing into a full-fledged sap, I was told that turkeys are so dumb that they would drown in the rain. I have never found anything that dumb. The wild turkey is a wily creature. Hunters find turkey hunting to be a great challenge.

One day, I was doing a radio show when a caller said that he had just seen his first wild turkey. I told him how cool that was, but he didn't share my enthusiasm. He had hit one with the windshield of the rental car he was driving. It shook him up so much that he had missed his turn.

Turkeys love to eat acorns. Because turkey teeth are as scarce as hen's teeth, turkeys have a modified muscular pouch behind the stomach called the gizzard that contains ingested grit that aids in the breakdown of seeds before digestion.

In case you are giving some thought to starting a used turkey-parts store, the snood is the fleshy appendage attached just above the bill. The caruncles are fleshy, bulbous bumps that grow over the head and neck. The dewlap connects the neck to the head just under the bill.

Every Thanksgiving my family eats copious amounts of turkey and then we have a group nap in front of a TV set showing a football game. I once put a tape in the VCR of a game from the year before. Nobody noticed. They slept as soundly as they would have during a live game.

My neighbor Crandall loves turkeys. He has seven of them. He keeps them in one of those little barns that you see behind home improvement centers. He calls it the House of Seven Gobbles.

One hot August day, my phone rang. It was Crandall. He told me that his turkeys were on the road and he was afraid that they might be run over by a big truck. I told him that I would be right over and that it would take no time whatsoever to round up the straying turkeys. I pontificated about them being birdbrains while we were the superior beings.

"Why spend time looking for a needle in the haystack when you could search for a turkey in the straw?" I said.

I joined Crandall in the chase. We quickly discovered that the birds could fly 55 miles per hour and run 25 miles per hour. They would run far ahead of us, stop and look back as if saying, "Are you coming? Let's go!" Then they did the turkey trot.

It was hot and so humid that fish swam by our heads. A neighbor caught a bullhead in a mousetrap. I was not only hot and sweaty; I was thirsty, hungry, tired, and grumpy. I had developed an intense dislike of Crandall's turkeys.

"I hope a big truck comes along and greases the entire flock," I said. "In my opinion, you'd be well rid of them."

My neighbor nodded glumly and we walked home.

The turkeys followed us home.

They were looking for leadership.

Outhouse Annals

Our bathroom wasn't allowed in the house. My father wasn't a fan of indoor bathrooms. He thought they were a passing fad that would never catch on. Our home had no indoor bathroom. It was uncanny. No one in our household ever uttered the words "Don't forget to jiggle the handle." Going to the bathroom in the middle of the night at the Batt house involved boots, a flashlight, and a second house. The best time to use the outhouse was during the noon hour because then all the flies were in the kitchen. Our outhouse was in the wrong place. Too close in the summer and too far away in the winter. No angry teenager in my family ever locked himself or herself in the bathroom. I'd whine in my most irritating voice, "Why don't we have an indoor outhouse?" Dad replied, "What if the house burned down? Then where would we go?"

That made sense to me. Whenever I'd read in a newspaper about someone's house burning down, I'd wonder where they were going. Father claimed that he was doing the family a favor by sticking with an outhouse. We didn't have much, but we'd always have a place to go.

Whenever I grumbled to Mother about having to go outside to use the toilet, she'd say "One day we'll have an indoor toilet." Mom said that in the manner that others say "One day we'll have world peace." Mom added that walking to the outhouse was good exercise and an outhouse was a great place to listen to the birds. Part of the "hole" experience was the avian chorus. I thought the outhouse was for the birds. The outhouse provided live entertainment. Spiders and wasps called it home. In the darkness, things that went bump in the night bumped in the night. Our outhouse was a three-holer. That was because we were rich. I'm not sure why we needed three holes. Maybe it was so we could give one another encouragement. Two of the holes were regulation-sized and one was smaller to fit the south end of a northbound child. Perhaps it was to promote spending quality time together. I'm all for family togetherness, but I never spent much time in there with Mom and Dad. A four-holer could have been a community-gathering place.

Mom called the outdoor toilet the "backhouse" or the "little house." Dad referred to it as the "Batt Library." It was the place he went to read the Old Farmer's Almanac or Zane Grey novels. The outhouse was Dad's sanctuary. The almanac hung from a string on a nail driven into the outhouse wall, positioned to distinguish it from the Sears catalog that served an important function in our outhouse. Yes, our toilet paper had page numbers. Staples could be dangerous, but we recycled. I could tell when company was coming. Mom put an extra leaf in the dining-room table and a new Sears catalog in the outhouse. The family was usually stuck with the dreaded slick pages. Kids today don't know what they're missing. You could cut diamonds with slick pages. We needed to crumple the slick pages many times before they were useable. Crumple them up, straighten them out. Repeat if necessary, and it would be necessary. It was more exercise.

We had neighbors who adored peaches. When nature not only called, but also put me on speed dial, it was worth a bicycle ride to their farm just to use the soft peach papers they kept in their outhouse. I retain a fondness for peaches to this day.

I called our outhouse the "easer." Anyone who has used an outhouse on a frigid January day will understand the nickname. You didn't just walk in and sit down. That's how heart attacks happen. You needed to ease your way down onto a seat edged in frost. There is an old saying, "Veni, vidi, Velcro." "I came, I saw, I stuck to it." You could do that in the winter. An outhouse could be grounds for child abuse today. I'd lie in bed when nature called until I nearly had a medical emergency before I was willing to get out of my warm bed, put on a coat and boots, and slog through snow to that darkened easer.

It had been a day with sprinkles on it. If you don't like sprinkles, it had been a day without sprinkles on it. Everything was copacetic. Then a plumbing problem arose. It stretched the definition of "plumbing," but it arose.

Clogged sink?

That's nothing.

Overflowing toilet?

A mere triviality, even if the toilet overflowed after you'd used it in the home of your boss who wasn't fond of you.

Mother charged into the house and said, "There's something in the outhouse. Get it out!"

Father wasn't always good at delegating authority, but he excelled at it that day. He told me to deal with the problem.

"Security!" I yelled, but none appeared.

I approached the outhouse with dread. I had no clue what was in it, but I suspected it wasn't pocket lint. It could have been a lion, tiger, or bear! Oh, my! It turned out to be a skunk that wasn't just in the biffy, it had found its way down into one of the holes.

I wished I'd been blessed with superpowers. Unfortunately, my only superpower was a great vulnerability to gravity.

A shudder ran up and down my spine as I considered methods of freeing the skunk.

I placed a board into the hole at an angle that would allow the skunk to climb upon it. Time passed like a stubborn kidney stone, but the skunk finally walked up the board.

The skunk was ingratiatingly polite as it ambled away from the outhouse. At least, I thought so until my nose detected a foul odor the skunk had left as a legacy.

Several years later, Mother charged into the house (she did that regularly) and said, "There's something in the outhouse. Get it out!"

Cue the violins.

I objected vehemently, but I was given the job because I had experience. Despite a fetid flashback, I was unable to decline the job. I was the go-to guy.

I trudged to the outhouse, mumbling to myself that life was unfair. I wondered where the skunk-removal board was.

I opened the door slowly in case it was an ambush. I prepared to take one for the team.

My spirits slumped significantly when I heard a soft sound.

A Life Gone to the Birds

Then a bluebird flew out. That bluebird of happiness carried my backhouse blues away.

I'd never been so happy to see a bird in my life.

Things that Go Boop Boop Shebop Bop in the Night

My niece Georgette shares my age.

When we were kids, one of my greatest pleasures was walking in the woods. It still is. It didn't matter if it were day or night; I wanted to tread lightly in treed land. A walk in the woods made me feel as though I were playing center field for the St. Louis Cardinals.

Georgette did not share this passion of mine, but my love for the woods was so great that my evangelistic glee would allow me to talk her into accompanying me on one of my epic adventures.

We walked into the middle of the 50 acres of woodlands and the barred owl would begin to call.

If you have ever heard anything in the woods that sounded like something you have never heard before, it was probably a barred owl.

This owl makes a monkey call that I find delightful.

Georgette found it terrifying. She ran home, her feet barely touching the ground.

I assured her that the owls were nothing to fear. The terrifying things in the woods were mosquitoes.

The Genius

I had considered becoming a lion tamer.

The hours were good, but I worried that I might lose my head with the job. Maybe a matador would be more fitting for a fellow like me. At least I wouldn't have to wear a necktie.

Then a favorite teacher told me that chickadees could be fed by hand. She added that chickadees were so small that three of them could be put in an envelope and mailed for a single first class stamp. She didn't tell me why I would mail chickadees. I don't know to whom I would mail three chickadees, but chickadees seemed as though they would be more fun to work with than hungry lions or angry bulls. My teacher's revelation was instant inspiration to me. My favorite bird in the whole wide world was the black-capped chickadee. I wasn't that old, but my admiration for the chickadee had been a lifelong one.

The chickadee is the Dale Carnegie or the Zig Ziglar of the avian world. Granted, the chickadee is smaller than Dale Carnegie or Zig Ziglar, and it has feathers, but otherwise they are exactly the same. The chickadee may be diminutive, but it has a positive attitude. Just like Mr. Carnegie, the chickadee makes friends and influences people. This tiny bird's *chick-a-dee-dee* call is among the best motivational speeches I have ever heard. It begins whistling *Spring's here* when our long winter's back is about to break. It is amazing the power housed in my feathered friend. The chickadee whistles *sweetie* and I feel wonderful. It whistles *love you* and I believe it.

I came up with a plan. We had a number of bird feeders hanging from the lilac bushes in our yard. I stacked a couple of straw bales near one of the feeder-laden lilacs. I procured a pitchfork with a broken handle (we had cornered the market on such broken things) and impaled the tines into one of the straw bales so that the short wooden handle protruded from the straw at an angle perpendicular to the ground. On the end of this pitchfork handle, I secured a yellowish Handy Andy work glove with baling twine. We didn't have any duct tape on the farm, but we did have an abundance of baling twine. The yellow glove was situated like a man's hand asking for a handout. Into this glove, I placed one of the chickadee's favorite foods—black-oil sunflower seeds.

This job done, I retreated to the kitchen of our old farmhouse and waited. I took up sentry duty by the window over our kitchen sink. I didn't have to wait long. Putting out sunflower seeds was like putting out sugar cookies for the relatives. The chickadees are a curious and hungry bunch—just like the relatives. The chickadees were the first to discover this new odd feeder. They visited often and regularly. Blue jays and nuthatches also became regular customers. For two weeks, I kept the gloved feeder filled. Then and only then was it time for my big experiment.

I was going to impress my family. This would be a difficult thing to accomplish. My family had seen me at my very worst. I gave them little choice.

I went outside and removed the straw bales. Then I put the yellowish Handy Andy work glove on my grimy little paw. I stood as still as possible for a boy my age, having perfected the ability that most men have of being able to do things without the necessity of having to think about anything. Men perfect this ability through hours of training otherwise known as fishing and watching televised sports. This comes in handy when a wife asks a husband what he is thinking, and he is truthfully able to reply, "Nothing."

I stood as motionless as a statue for as long as it took.

Before long, the chickadees came to feed from my gloved hand. They came one at a time according to a determined pecking order. Tiny black eyes checked me out and determined I was harmless and that parts of me were edible. Occasionally, a nuthatch stopped by for a snack. The chickadees were great to work with. They never growled or pawed the ground while snorting and they never complained about a meal.

My mother had me perform my little hand-feeding trick whenever relatives came by for a visit. Mom broke out the rosettes and coffee strong enough to stir itself, and fed the multitudes. Meanwhile, I'd be standing outside with a yellow glove on my hand awaiting the arrival of the chickadees. Mom directed everyone's attention my way. The members of my family tried to ignore her, but my mother would have none of that. She was adamant about their need to look at me. My relatives gathered around the kitchen window and watched in amazement as a chickadee landed on my gloved hand.

A hush fell over the crowd. It was a small hush. No injuries.

"Look!" they'd cry, spitting out remnants of rosettes in their excitement. "He's trained those little birds to eat right out of his hands!"

My Uncle Vern was the first to suggest it. "You know what the boy is?" he said.

There were a number of guesses.

Uncle Vern said, "He's a genius."

No one had guessed that. No one had come even close to guessing that.

"That explains why he's so odd. I thought he was just strange. You know, a dork," came several responses.

It was apparent. I had moved from being dumber than a bag of hammers to being a genius, thanks to a chickadee.

My mother and my family were in agreement—I was a genius. That was the consensus.

It remained so, until my report card arrived.

How Do You Mend a Broken Wing?

I was standing in the kitchen of our old farmhouse.

I had to stand because sitting caused me to think I was missing something.

I was drinking a glass of Tang, because it was what the astronauts drank.

I was at the age where I was on the verge of knowing everything.

I looked out the window over the sink towards the lilacs. My ancestors built barns so they would have work, then they built houses so they would have shade. Then they marked their territories by planting lilacs. Inside the house, women marked their territories with doilies.

I was quaffing a delicious genuine imitation orange juice and looking at lilacs.

We fed the birds. My father made bird feeders and placed them about the yard. I constructed the occasional feeder. Having only a vague understanding of the workings of a hammer, my productions were those of the carpentry-impaired, but the birds didn't seem to mind and graciously accepted the offerings.

I watched chickadees feed. I love chickadees. I want to do for them what Florence did for the nightingales. Chickadees have a spirit so fierce that if they were the size of a chicken, none of us would dare go outdoors.

My eyes moved to a small brown bird fluttering on the ground.

I was sharper than a pocketful of toothpicks in those days, so I knew instantly that the bird was injured.

The old gospel song said, "His eye is on the sparrow."

I put down my glass of Tang and went outside. After some effort, I was able to apprehend the injured bird. It was a female house sparrow, also called an English sparrow. Other folks were known to refer to them as "spatzies" or "sputzies." Still others called them names I could not repeat here.

I brought the bird into the house and put it into an old

parakeet cage. We hadn't had a budgie in the house for many years, so the space was available.

The sparrow didn't take well to being incarcerated, but she was safe from cats and other predators.

I fed the little hen Wonder Bread. I thought it would be just the thing for a tiny bird that appeared to have a broken wing. Why Wonder Bread? Well, it helped build strong bodies 12 different ways.

After a couple of days, the bird calmed down in my presence, either because I brought her food, she knew I was trying to help her, or she realized that she was intellectually my superior.

I fed, watered, cleaned, and generally cared for my little patient for two weeks. She appeared to be improving. She chirped constantly, the little sound that has made the sparrow a favorite in English gardens.

I decided that the sparrow should be released back into the wild. My parents encouraged this. I'll never forget what my father said about the sparrow. I'll never forget. No, sir, I'll never forget that. Well, OK, I forgot what he said, but it was good—trust me.

I had named the bird Marilyn. I had begun to appreciate Marilyn Monroe and I didn't care if she could act or not.

One day, my parents were off to town. I was left home alone without adult supervision. My father had given me his usual admonition before leaving. "Try not to burn the house down while we're gone."

Boy, you burn one house down and you're branded for life.

I thought the absence of my parents presented the perfect opportunity to set Marilyn free. My reasoning was that if I got weepy during the release, at least my parents wouldn't be able to see the major crack in my manly exterior.

My plan was to climb to the top of the windmill. My

mother disliked the windmill because of her youngest child's insistence on climbing it.

I took the little bird from her cage and talked kindly to her. As I used one hand to climb the ladder to the top of the windmill, I kept reassuring the tiny creature that everything would be okay.

I reached the top of the windmill. There was an undersized platform just under the spinning blades of the windmill that was a perfect place for a young boy to sit.

I held the little bird as I gave her some tips on living and then I wished her the best of what life offers as I tossed her into the air.

My experience with that little sparrow taught me so much.

I learned that putting a little bird into a parakeet's cage and feeding it Wonder Bread for two weeks does not mend a broken wing.

Barn Swallows

I watched an old movie, *Mr. Hobbs Takes a Vacation*, starring Jimmy Stewart in the title role. Hobbs was coerced into going "bird spotting" with his son-in-law's boss, Mr. Turner. Each time the inexperienced Hobbs thought he'd spotted a new bird and asked for an identification, Turner gave him a sneeringly dismissive, "Barn swallow." The great Chinese philosopher Chuang Tzu would not have agreed with Turner's attitude, as he wrote, "There is no bird wiser than the swallow."

Years ago, when I milked cows, pairs of barn swallows would return every year and build their nests inside the barn. The door to the barn remained open during the day from May to September. The swallows had a family to raise. The swallows treated the comings and goings of the cows, dogs, and humans with great tolerance. Everybody got along just fine. By summer, the heads of three or four chicks would appear over the rim of the muddy nest, and whenever a parent returned with a meal, the chicks would open their mouths and strain their necks skyward like choirboys singing. The elegance of those barn swallows as they carved the sky overhead brought us joy and their annual arrival marked time in our lives. The swallows embroidered the world around us and made our lives richer. They were hope on the wing. Shakespeare wrote, "Hope is swift and flies on swallow's wings."

The Five Ducks

What makes a man a birder?

I know.

They were strange ducks.

And I know strange ducks. I guess that's why they liked to hang around with me. Birds of a feather flock together.

They were strange ducks and they were not the most attractive ducks to set webbed foot on the earth. A Muscovy duck is not the Brad Pitt or the Jennifer Anniston of the waterfowl world. We had a lot of them (the ducks, not Pitts or Annistons) on the farm while I was growing up. They multiplied like feathered rabbits. They were Bible-reading ducks. They got to the part where it said, "be fruitful and multiply" and then they had no more time for reading. The odd-looking ducks had red faces and a habit of making puffing and hissing sounds whenever anyone got close to them. Many of these ducks had taken up residence in our dairy barn.

One morning, I had just finished milking the cows and had tiptoed my way through the gathering of ducks begging for food by the Dutch doors on the front of the barn. I stepped outside, shutting the doors behind me. I had walked but a few feet when a Muscovy drake came sailing in. These ducks were decent flyers and they could glide a good distance, but they weren't equipped with much for brakes. They were not unlike the rare bent-billed duck. A rapid flyer but not good at stopping. The duck obviously hadn't noticed that the barn door was closed. The poor old drake hit the door like a June bug hitting the windshield of a Buick. It bounced off the door and hit the ground with a sickening thud. I picked the duck up, expecting it to be a dead duck. I was surprised to notice a bit of life in the duck, so I set it inside the barn on a bale of straw. When I came back later to check on the Evel Knievel of duckdom, I discovered that it was very much alive and appeared none the worse for the experience. It was then that an idea formed in my teenage brain.

I had the occasional idea in those days—my friends and family referred to them as "brain cramps." I shared my idea with my best friend, Crandall. He was not always enthralled with my ideas. He claimed that I didn't have ideas, I had schemes. Schemes that failed to produce anything but detention hours. I explained to Crandall that my sister had just been to a convention and that she had a pile of those, "Hello, My Name Is..." nametags with the sticky backs left over and that I had an overabundance of Muscovy ducks. I laid out the rest of my plan and insisted that it would turn us into legends.

First, we caught four of the big ducks. Then we used a black magic marker to fill out four of those nametags. On the first, we printed "Duck Number One." We wrote on the other three so that we ended up with four nametags and put one each on a wing of the four ducks. The nametags read, "Hello, I'm Duck Number One," "Hello, I'm Duck Number Two," "Hello, I'm Duck Number Three" and "Hello, I'm Duck Number Five."

We placed the ducks gently into the trunk of my dilapidated Ford and drove to Keyman's house. We listened to pulsating rock and roll on WDGY Radio as we cackled fiendishly at the genius of our wicked plan. The radio worked better than any other part of the car. Keyman's father was a custodian at the local high school that Crandall and I attended, although all our records have mysteriously disappeared. Keyman, in an obvious concern for the well-being of his fellow man, had had a duplicate key made of every one of the 219 keys that were on his father's key ring. He did this in case some kind of disaster struck. If such a calamity happened, Keyman would have been able to open all the doors and free the students trapped in a burning or collapsing school with nothing to eat but school lunches. Crandall and I asked Keyman if it would be possible for us to borrow a key to the door of the school. Keyman was more than willing to help. What a guy. Under the cover of darkness on a Sunday night, Crandall and I opened the gigantic front door of the school—it was the size of a drawbridge—and released ducks number one, two, three, and five into the institute of learning.

I found it difficult to sleep that night. I tossed and turned. Then I turned and tossed.

When Crandall and I arrived at school the next morning, we found the place in an uproar. Everyone was in a tizzy. Some folks were even in a dither. School administrators, teachers, lunchroom ladies, and custodians were all scrambling about like chickens with their heads cut off.

"What is going on?" I asked our high school principal with as much innocence as I could muster.

"Oh," he growled, "some idiot let some critters loose in the school."

"Critters, you say. What kind of critters?" I asked, pretending to be wearing a halo.

"I've never seen anything like them, but they are ducks," he said.

"How do you know?" I continued my inquisition.

"Because they wore a label identifying them as ducks. This was obviously the dastardly deed of somebody with too much time on his hands. This idiot, and I might be giving him too much credit for his intelligence, labeled the critters. We found duck number one, two, and three near the chemistry lab and we found duck number five on top of the trophy showcase, staring down with evil intent at the stuffed barred owl, but we are still looking for that fourth duck. I'm telling you boys right now that school will not start until we find that fourth duck. "

I smirked. I didn't mean to. I couldn't help it. I was a teenager.

The principal glared at me and said, "And if I find out that you had something to do with this, you will be looking for strange birds until we find that fourth duck!"

And as far as I know, they are still looking for duck number four.

And I am still looking for birds—strange or otherwise.

A Life Gone to the Birds

Chapter 2:
No One Has Accused
Me of Being an Adult

Cartoon Birds

It's a bird, it's a plane! Maybe it's time to get my eyes checked. No, it's the perfect excuse to get new binoculars.

"Look, up in the sky, it's a bird, it's a plane, it's a frog—a frog? Not bird, nor plane, nor even frog, it's just little ol' me, Underdog!"

Nearly every birder keeps a bird list of some kind—life, annual, country, state, county, yard, airport, zoo, etc. A list of flying canines would be good, but I keep a list of cartoon/comic birds.

My list contains Donald Duck, Daffy Duck, Woody Woodpecker, Tweety Bird, Foghorn Leghorn, Baby Huey, Tennessee Tuxedo, Huey, Dewey and Louie, Super Chicken, Scrooge McDuck, Road Runner, Heckle and Jeckle, Henery Hawk, Darkwing Duck, Opus, Quackula, Beaky Buzzard, Plucky Duck, Birdman, Howard the Duck, Chilly Willy, Count Duckula, Hawkman, Duckman, Destroyer Duck, Spacehawk, Toucan Sam, Daisy Duck, Mallard Fillmore, Mother Goose, Shoe, Woodstock, Cosmo Fishhawk, Loon, and Dinky Duck.

I'm missing some, but that's a good thing. I'll have to keep looking.

The Bird Walk

I led a spring bird walk for beginning birders one year.

The day we picked turned out to be an unfortunate choice. It was cold, windy, and the rain poured down. I polled the participants, asking if they wanted to brave the elements to bird. They agreed unanimously. We walked and saw good birds. At the end of the hour-long stroll, we gathered in a dry shelter and I thanked everyone for his or her good company. A drenched man told me, "I see why you love birding. It feels good when you stop."

It's Morning Either Way

I was speaking at gatherings in Gulf Shores, Alabama. I went birding each morning while I was there. The white sand, warm weather, and birds made for delightful walks.

Early one morning, I walked by a table situated outside a large hotel and encountered a man enjoying an adult beverage. I hoped it was his first of the day. He asked me what I was doing. I told him that I was looking at birds. He grimaced and said, "Awfully early in the morning for that kind of thing, isn't it?"

The Indigo Bunting

My wife's favorite bird is the indigo bunting. It looks like a blue goldfinch. I watched a lovely indigo bunting at the feeder. As it flew away, I was reminded of the last words in a novel, *Jitterbug Perfume*, written by Tom Robbins. "As blue as indigo. And you know what that means: Indigo. Indigoing. Indigone."

Avian Larceny

Once upon a time, I was laboring over the delicate inner workings of an Allis-Chalmers tractor under the spreading maple tree near my home. My village smithy activities were interrupted as I watched a crow fly down and steal a very small open-end wrench.

He flew away while I ran after him, shouting in protest.

Just as I am, crows are attracted to small, shiny objects.

I had hoped that the corvid had only borrowed the wrench for some chore he was doing and that he would be returning it.

I'm still waiting. I had to borrow a wrench to finish my task.

Stuck with Birds

I headed up the steep and icy driveway to some friends' house.

I was driving my pickup. It was a great vehicle, but one with slippery feet.

It was a cold, cold day—15 degrees below zero.

I was journeying up one of those drives that are so steep and icy that you have to give your vehicle plenty of foot in order to make it to the top where their house sits.

I think of myself as a much better driver than I am and have a comfort level on winter roads that I do not deserve.

I floored it and was making the climb without any problem when I happened to notice something fly from the large feeder in front of the house.

I put my foot on the brake and grabbed my binoculars. Red crossbills! Not a rare bird, but certainly not a common bird in my area. There was a small flock of the beautiful birds.

I was enjoying watching the flock of birds through my binoculars when suddenly I had that odd feeling. That strange feeling that I was moving while sitting in place. And moving I was. I was sliding down the long drive. I pressed my foot down on the gas pedal, but all that accomplished was nothing. I tried to steer in order to stay on the road. I tried pumping the brakes, but to no avail. I slid until I went into a ditch filled with rock hard snow. I tried to drive out of the ditch, but had no luck.

I got out of my truck, walked to the house at the top of the hill, and discovered that no one was home. I borrowed a shovel from their garage and tried to move some snow from around my truck. The shovel was meant for pushing snow, not for shoveling snow. All I accomplished was chipping bits of snow off the banks, slipping on the hard-packed snow, and banging my ear on the box of my pickup.

Several people, those hardy folks who walk even on the coldest days, stopped to offer advice—I should make sure to bend my knees, I should learn to stay home on such days like this, etc. A man said that what I was doing was woman's work and that I should call my wife. A very nice woman feeding her horses nearby offered me encouragement. I shoveled more energetically with a cheerleader nearby. The horses gave me sympathetic looks, realizing that I was one dumb animal.

I shoveled for about an hour, accomplishing nothing more than getting my pickup deeper into the ditch. I gave up.

Using the cell phone, I tried calling several friends who lived in the vicinity and had 4-wheel drive pickups or farm tractors. Large pickups or tractors could free me from my predicament with little cost and only a slight loss of pride.

Nobody was home at any of the numbers I called.

As frugal as I am, I was finally forced to call a tow truck. The tow boys were having a busy day, so it took them 45 minutes to get there.

When the cavalry arrived, the hill was so icy that it took the tow truck a dozen runs to get to the top. He hooked up a cable to the pickup, but was unable to pull it out of the ditch because of the ice. He needed to go to the next drive, run a long cable to my vehicle, and pull it out sideways. The driver was very pleasant, worked very hard, and after another 45 minutes, I was a free man. Well, free except for the $50 I had to pay him. I realize that $50 was cheap compared to spending the rest of my life in that ditch.

I drove down the road. My truck dropped bits of packed snow. I knew that I was back on the road and that I was willing and able to traverse the obstacles the day's roads would place in front of me, but I knew just how Jack Benny felt after paying $50 and having nothing to show for it.

But you know what—it was all worth it. I did have something to show for my trials and tribulations. I had the pleasure of having seen the beautiful crossbills.

Life presents gifts to us to help us make the tough times bearable.

My wife thinks I am nuts—her friends and family agree with her. So does everyone in her therapy group. She even claims that Doctor Phil is on her side on this one.

Watch for me on an upcoming *Jerry Springer Show* titled, "My Husband is a Birder."

How Cold was It?

It was so cold that I could get an ice cream headache without eating ice cream.

I was doing a Christmas Bird Count on one of Minnesota's coldest winter days. Below zero temperatures may not look like much on an old mercury thermometer advertising Benson's Welding Shop, but they can chill a birder.

We were looking for birds. There were three of us. I was in the company of two young fellows. They were sharp, college students—whippersnappers. We walked through a park and stopped to look at a wood duck box attached to a tree. The edges of the entrance hole had been gnawed.

The young fellows asked me if there might be a screech-owl in the box. I admitted that it was possible, but that the resident was more likely a squirrel. I based my answer on the gnawed entrance. The young guys, with more ambition than I possessed, decided that one of them would climb onto the shoulders of the other and peer into the wood duck box. I decided to limit my involvement and backed away. I wanted to give them room to operate while avoiding any calamity that might ensue.

What happened next was just like the movie *True Grit* only completely different.

With a minimum of grumbling and groaning, one man climbed onto the back of the other, slowly making his way to the shoulders of his support group of one. The combination stood, gathering stability. They looked as if they were some kind of cheap halftime entertainment. They wobbled close to the tree and the top half leaned towards the nest box.

He looked into the hole. Something looked back at him.

A frightened gray squirrel jumped from the wood duck box, bouncing off the top man's head. The squirrel had found the fellow's melon blocking his escape route. The top man made a sound that I had never heard before. He tipped over. The bottom man made yet another new sound for my ears. He tipped as well. The men fell to their backs with a muffled thud onto a ground covered with snow. They both grunted in response to the impact. Then one or both of them might have said something like, "Cheese and crackers!" They made unintentional snow angels as they rolled around like participants in a sack race who had just lost to the sack.

I calculated their frequent faller miles. I wanted to yell "Timber!" at the men who stare at squirrels, but I withheld my vocalization until I could be sure my partners in the bird counting game were unhurt.

THIS BOOK BELONGS TO

AND

CARRIES THE GOOD WISHES OF

BIRD WATCHER'S DIGEST • BOX 110 • MARIETTA, OHIO • BIRDWATCHERSDIGEST.COM

The squirrel on the other hand, had no time to lie down on the job. It scurried up the same tree from which it had leaped. It hit a branch of the evergreen that held a bough covered with a generous amount of snow. As it bounced further up the tree, the snow fell from the bough down onto the faces of my two fallen compadres.

Eleven out of ten doctors do not recommend snow on the face and down the neck on a frigid day. It hastened my associates' return to upright positions. We walked quickly to the car. As quickly as three men, two of whom looked like they had just eaten Vaseline sandwiches, could walk. The windchill served to make a cold day one of a "Frost-bite Falls" quality. The incident would have made a perfect spot on *The Weather Channel*.

We warmed up in the car. I thawed some hot soup. The heater's work made my birding buddies as giddy as Donald Trump at a toupee sale.

I might have mumbled, "Timber," a little louder than I should have.

I hope the two men have forgiven me by the next Christmas Bird Count.

The Attack

Hartland is a quiet town.

Mal Content occasionally lets his bagpipes squeal just enough to put fear into the town's teenage population, but the typical hush is what makes this tale intriguing.

This story was related to me by David Harleyson. Names and facts have been changed to enhance the story.

David Harleyson was out for a ride on his Harley-Davidson. He'd never recovered from seeing the movie, *Easy Rider*. David had reached the age where he still respected his elders—they were just harder to find. David knew his way around town. The irony of life is that by the time you're old enough to know your way around, you're not going anywhere. He liked to ride every street in town. Not much of a task. First Street is on the edge of town.

David passed under the big maple that had just enough elm in its family tree to have contracted Dutch Elm Disease. He never imagined that cruising on a motorcycle through a residential neighborhood could be dangerous.

As David dreamed of high speeds on long, straight roads, a furry package fell from the old tree and landed with a thump on David's shoulder.

This transported David's mind from Sturgis to Hartland.

David screamed as if he had experience. If David would've had hiccups, he'd have been cured.

The squirrel screamed, too. David had never heard such language from a rodent. The squirrel began to rip and tear at David's black T-shirt advertising Bergdale Harley.

As the two continued their ride at slow speeds, David attempted to seize his tormentor. He grabbed the squirrel's tail and flipped the beast into the air.

David didn't have time for a cleansing breath before, with a snarl befitting a grizzly bear with a toothache, the squirrel fell from the sky and landed on David's head.

David swore that he heard Rod Serling's voice saying, "There is a fifth dimension beyond that which is known to man. It is a dimension as vast as space and as timeless as infinity. It is the middle ground between light and shadow, between science and superstition, and it lies between the pit of man's fears and the summit of his knowledge. This is the dimension of imagination. It is an area which we call the Twilight Zone."

The squirrel attached itself to David's face like one of those Garfield dolls to a car window. The squirrel had a lot of anger.

Picture a large man on a motorcycle puttering along at 15 mph down a quiet residential street with a squirrel holding a firm grip on the man's mug. As David used one hand in an attempt to dislodge his attacker, his other hand inadvertently gave a twist to the throttle. This didn't improve the situation.

Suddenly a large man with a squirrel plastered to his face was roaring 50 mph on a motorcycle through a residential neighborhood. The sound of the Harley's engine drowned out by the screams of man and squirrel.

The acceleration forced David to put both hands on the handlebars in order to control the big bike. Because the squirrel made a better door than a window, David saw only a tiny bit of the street.

The squirrel, using its keen animal instincts to realize that a high-speed collision with a parked car or large tree would likely not do a squirrel any good, climbed down from David's face and found a hiding place inside David's black T-shirt.

By this point, David had lost his ability to scream, but his faculty for thought had returned. David reached under his T-shirt, snatched the squirrel by the tail, and having learned his lesson, flung the bushytail to the side instead of up.

Now picture yourself as a package deliveryman. You're just getting back into your brown van after dropping off a package for a homeowner. As you sit down, you feel a breeze as though something had flown past your head. You blame it on overwork.

David pulled his Harley to the side of the street. He'd just gotten his heart restarted when he looked up to see a large delivery van headed his way.

He heard screams coming from the van. One of the screams sounded like that of a man. The other sounded even more familiar. As the van zoomed past, David wondered if the driver was wearing a beard or had a squirrel on his face.

Hartland is a quiet town.

Witnesses still talk about David Harleyson's motorcycle ride and the missing brown delivery van driven by a man with the face of a squirrel.

I'm Gullible

The farmer brought me a gull. It had flown into the window of the cab on the man's tractor.

Glass is like Kryptonite to a gull.

The ag-head thought the gull was a goner. He threw it into his pickup. He was going to check a field guide for identification. The gull came to in the truck. It flopped around a bit, but didn't appear to be able to fly.

My morning had not yet shed its training wheels when the farmer brought the bird to me because he thought that I needed a gull.

I live in flyover land—not just for people from New York and Los Angeles, or just for black helicopters, but for gulls as well. Gulls do spend time here before their arrival at their destinations (lakes). They follow tractors that are busily altering the landscape. The gulls eat the grubs and other goodies the tractors free from the soil.

I was not then nor am I now a licensed wildlife rehabilitator (I don't even play one on TV), but sometimes a man has to do what a man has to do—as long as his wife hasn't told him otherwise.

My need for an injured gull wasn't that great, but I don't know how to be uninvolved. I took the gull gift in the spirit that it was given. I sympathized with the bird as I have walked into a glass patio door. It stung like the dickens.

Curse that effective glass cleaner.

I didn't know the sex of the bird, but I declared him a male based on his many disgusting habits. I named him Jethro Gull. The name meant nothing to the gull, as he wasn't going to come no matter what I called him. He had a personality. Not unlike that weird cousin we all have with the cantankerous disposition who is confused by the plot twists in a Bugs Bunny cartoon. Gulls have a reputation of being noisy creatures, but this one was a good listener.

I rigged up an old pigeon cage and the gull moved about his large for most birds, but small for him cage. It was a bed and breakfast for a gull. He was always happy to see me unless I didn't bring food. I didn't have any Purina Gull Chow on hand, but fortunately a gull will eat pretty much anything. I fed the gull some Wonder Bread—because it helps build strong bodies 12 different ways. I gave him corn and various kinds of large insects.

We bonded. I became more of a gull than I had been. This was a big improvement. The gull became more of a human—a possible step backwards for the bird.

The gull thrived. His strength returned. I think it was the Wonder Bread that did the trick. Jethro became very vocal. I don't speak gull and his English wasn't the best, but I concluded that he wanted to be returned to the wild. I examined his wings. They seemed to be in good shape. I reasoned that the gull's problems could have been psychosomatic. He thought he couldn't fly. I read books to the gull about the power of positive thinking. I made the determination that I would release him near the site of the accident. Free Gully.

I drove my pickup, with the caged gull in the back, to the field where the gull had been injured. I have no doubt that Jethro considered it a return to the scene of the crime.

I opened the door of the cage. The gull did not venture out hesitatingly. He bolted through the exit and took flight. He circled over my head. Actually he figure-eighted over my head, squawking loudly.

The field wasn't far from my house. For a few weeks, the bird would fly in and squawk until I fed him. He would figure-eight over my head. He made an odd sound that I didn't hear from other gulls. He became my buddy. He would dip his right wing as a signal before landing upon my shoulder and nuzzling my ear. He whispered sweet nothings in my ear. He must have known that I had saved his life.

Then one day, he didn't show up. I assumed he had migrated. I missed him.

Nearly a year passed. That's what nearly all years do. Then one day, I was walking to my pickup, when I heard that odd squawking. I looked up and there was a gull doing a figure-eight over my head. Jethro! I rejoiced.

It flew closer and I smiled as I readied myself for my old friend to land on my shoulder.

It didn't land on my shoulder.

It pooped right in my eye.

It probably wasn't Jethro.

Binoculars

One of the great joys of my life is being able to lead field trips looking at birds, flowers, trees, mammals, and anything else in nature. Leading children around a state park is a particular joy to me.

There is nothing quite like seeing something through the eyes of a child who is seeing it for the first time. I never cease to marvel at their enthusiasm and willingness to express their awe.

I walked with a group of 5th graders at Myre-Big Island

State Park. There were numerous scarlet tanagers in the Park that day and I wanted to make sure every one of my charges got a good look at these beautiful birds. A scarlet tanager male, with his bright red and lovely black colors, is an "Ahhh Bird." Whenever anyone sees one of these birds through binoculars or a spotting scope, they cannot help but issue an, "Ahhh."

This day, I was leading 15 kids in a group. I had brought along eight binoculars for the kids to use. The idea was that they would share the optics. It was a good idea—and like many good ideas, it was better in theory than in practice. But the kids were great. That's because kids are great. Every generation of adults says the same thing: "What's the matter with the kids today? Why can't they be like we were—perfect in every way?" I want to tell everyone that there is nothing wrong with the kids today. Society may have some problems, but the kids are wonderful.

The kids were using the binoculars as you might expect them to. They were looking at the heads of other kids and saying, "Ew! Cooties!" They would turn the binoculars around so they were looking through the big lenses at their feet saying, "This is what my feet would look like if I were 30 feet tall."

They did find the time to see the birds. The tanagers worked their magic on the children. The kids made sounds as if they were seeing fireworks when they spotted a tanager. I wondered if one of them would become hooked on birds as I am. I had hoped that each child would see a tanager and my hopes were fulfilled—every child had a good look at the tanagers.

As our hike continued, a girl by the name of Becky began to walk beside me. She was bubbling. "These are the greatest binoculars I have ever seen!" she gushed. "Why, I'm seeing things I've never seen before. These have to be the best binoculars in the world."

I guessed they were the only binoculars she had ever peered through. I appreciated her enthusiasm—no one values optics and their magic more than I do, but the binoculars were far from being the best in the world. They were well worn from years of constant use.

She asked me where I had gotten the binoculars. I told Becky the story on how I came to possess those glasses. When I was 11 years old, I was given a bird book published by *Capper's Weekly*. It was a tremendous book. It was a pleasure to be able to put a name to the birds I was seeing and hearing. Shortly after getting this book, I made the decision to become the "Birdman" of Hartland, Minnesota. There seemed to be an opening in that position. There was only one thing preventing me from becoming the "Birdman:" I had no binoculars. What kind of a "Birdman" could I be without binoculars?

I started making subtle hints. I cut binocular ads from my brother's *Field & Stream*, *Outdoor Life*, and *Sports Afield* magazines and left them lying about the house where my mother would see them. I nailed a couple of the ads to the walls of our outhouse. I had decided to concentrate my campaign on my mother, as she was much more likely to succumb to my pleadings than was my father.

Mother would say something like, "I wonder who that is going up Joe Holland's driveway?" Joe was a neighbor.

"I don't know," I'd reply. "But I'll bet if I had a pair of binoculars, I could tell you."

My persistent, understated approach worked. My mother, with money she did not have, went to Montgomery Ward's and bought me binoculars on the layaway plan. Dad complained about money being spent at "Monkey Ward's," but Mom prevailed. I don't know how long it took her to come up with the necessary funds, but one day she presented me with a gift that I had hoped and prayed for. I loved my mother even more than usual, if that were possible, that day. It sounds hokey to say so, but those binoculars changed my life. Just as Becky had, I began seeing things that I had never seen before. Once I finished my story, I looked down at Becky.

"I hope…," she started to say.

Oh, I knew what she was going to say. She was going to say that she hoped her mother would buy her binoculars. Or that she hoped her father would buy them for her. Or maybe, if she was as I was at her age, she'd say, "I hope you give these to me."

She didn't say any of these things. What Becky said was, "I hope that when I grow up and I have a little boy, that I buy him some binoculars just like these."

Suddenly, I had tears in my eyes. This little girl had learned something that takes most of us a lifetime to learn, if we ever learn it. Becky knew that what we carry with us all the days of our lives is not what we grab and accumulate along the way. What we carry with us is what we do for and give to others.

My mother told me that I could never lose what I gave away. Becky told me that my mother was right.

Warbler Neck

"A birdie with a yellow bill / hopped upon the window sill. / Cocked his shining eye and said / 'What's that in the road? A head?'"

I laugh at this corrupted version of an old Robert Louis Stevenson poem that was recited often on an old TV show called *Axel and his Dog* that emanated from the studios of Channel 4 in a faraway place called the Twin Cities—Minneapolis and St. Paul.

My wife groans. She's heard my rendition often.

"I'm off birding," I chirp to my lovely bride.

"You're off in a lot of other ways, too," is her reply. She's a real card.

I spit on my handkerchief and wipe my binoculars. It's family tradition. It's the way my mother washed my face.

Thomas Carlyle advised, "Stop a moment, cease your work, and look around you." I do him one better. I stop before I even begin any work. The Three Stooges would be proud of me.

I hope to see many warblers on this day. I remember the line from the movie *The Shawshank Redemption*: "Remember, Red, hope is a good thing, maybe the best of things."

I drive to a county park and walk to a location known to produce good looks at the feather jewels. Birding is a combination of three sports—hiking, voyeurism, and hoping. Boxing is the sweet science. Birding is the tweet science.

I hear whisperings of birds far removed. The songs become louder as I walk. Every male bird thinks he's Barry White.

There is a group of folks there. A field trip in search of avian delights. This is good. The warblers deserve a parade.

I assume the warbler-watching position—feet spread comfortably, binoculars tipped towards the tops of the trees as though I am looking for clouds shaped like birds. I scan a tree filled with varicolored warblers. It's a morning of which a birder's dreams are made. Some look on it as an odd activity, but watching birds isn't odd. People watch golf and fishing on TV. That's odd. Looking at birds isn't enough. You have to stare at them. Each one is a definite flight risk.

I listen to the ongoing color commentary.

"See the bird?"

"Where?"

"That's a good bird."

"What's a good bird?"

It's like the Birder's Tourette's syndrome. "What is it? Where is it? Where did it go?"

"There it is in that green tree. It's at 5 o'clock. Now it's at 9 o'clock. Now it's about 9 minutes to 5."

"A green tree. Is it that ash? One of the maples? Or that big oak?"

"I think so."

"You do know what a tree looks like, don't you?"

"Is that it singing?"

"Trees don't sing!"

"I mean the bird."

"There are a lot of birds singing. Which song are you talking about?"

"I thought I didn't hear the bird over there, but actually, I'm not hearing it over here."

"Is that the bird on that dead branch?"

"Which dead branch?"

"The one with the bird on it."

"Oh, that's not the bird. That's not even a bird."

"Is that the tree you're talking about? The one with all of the leaves?"

"That's the one."

"There is more than one bird in that tree."

"Are we looking at the same bird?"

"The bird is hard to see when you're looking for it. This one is sort of green with white wing bars."

"Oh, it's a different bird. The one I'm looking at is green, but it has white wing bars."

"Where is it?"

"Right here in my binoculars. That's the best I can do without using a paint gun."

"See that? I didn't either."

"Oh, I see it, but a bird like that does not exist."

"The bird doesn't change while you're looking at it. You must have missed an episode of *Wild Kingdom*."

"It's not rocket science. It's more difficult than that."

"Take the training wheels off your binoculars. Trying to show you that bird is like trying to teach calculus to Gilligan."

It's short-attention-span birding. It's *Mad Magazine*'s idea of birding. Birders are capable of having lengthy conversations that are meaningless to others.

It's the greatest show on earth. Watching warblers is like seeing celebrities. I want to tell them that I really enjoy their work. I bird today because of what I saw yesterday and because of what I will see tomorrow.

A field-guide-thumbing, binocular-toting friend of mine joins us. We grunt a howdy in one another's direction. He has new Swarovski binoculars, a Zeiss spotting scope, and a rusty 1981 Ford pickup with 312,679 miles on it. I can smell stale coffee and doughnuts on his breath. Seeing him causes memories of our old garage band that we almost started, The Yellow-rumped Warblers, to touch delicately a remaining brain cell or two.

My friend quotes Calvin of *Calvin and Hobbes* comic strip fame, "When birds burp it must taste like bugs."

"I spy with my little eye," I say. For a moment, I don't care what kind of warblers they are. I'm just glad they are there. If I owned a baseball team, I'd name them the Warblers. The warblers remind me that I'll remain a happy camper as long as I keep looking at birds with a beginner's eyes.

My friend is working on a birding component system. It finds the bird, it identifies the bird, it takes a photo of the bird, it sends documentation to all who require it, and makes a phone call to everyone he has ever met carrying binoculars. Until he perfects it, we sort out the birds with learned identification skills.

I have a friend who is a chiropractor. Chiropractic is a noble profession involving bending and cracking that practitioners call "adjusting." This chiropractor loves warblers. He thinks that at least one of them ought to be the state bird. Oh, he enjoys seeing them, but he doesn't look at them that often. He's busy bending and cracking folks. What he appreciates about warblers is the business they bring him.

There is a reason some people would rather look at elephants and whales instead of warblers. Warbler watchers look up until we contract it: Warbler neck.

The neck becomes stiff and sore. A palm of the hand pressing on the back of the neck is a badge of honor that identifies warbler watchers. Warbler neck is a small price to pay for a look at a beautiful bird.

Buying Used Binoculars

I live on a farm near Hartland, Minnesota.

You don't see many people around Hartland wearing suits outside of church.

It's just not something that a Hartlander does. And there is a good reason why he doesn't often wear a suit. A fellow wearing a suit in Hartland anywhere but within shouting distance of clergy usually hears the same thing: "Will the defendant please rise?" This kind of thing can put a man off suits entirely.

I have a suit. It's a nice suit that I've owned long enough that it has gone in and out of style several times. I wear it to church doings and when I pretend to be a burned-out, high-powered executive. I have many neckties. For Christmas and Father's Day, I get neckties. I have a lovely pair of wingtip shoes made of good leather. I baby them because I know how much a cow sacrificed in order to keep me well-shod. I polish those shoes before I put them on. I clean them before the shoes are once again relegated to the confines of the closet.

My wife says that I look good in a suit. Folks have been known to comment, "You clean up real good."

Once upon a time, my family was invited to a relative's wedding in Iowa. It was a ceremony that I felt a need to attend. Knowing that half of all marriages end in divorce, I try to make half of the weddings I'm invited to. We finished the work that had to be done because there is always work that has to be done and we got ourselves all slicked up. I was wearing my suit and my lovely bride was attired in her posh frock. I put on a tie, even though wearing a necktie puts a kink in my day. It makes me feel as if I were tied to a fencepost.

I was on a mission that day. I had discovered the existence of some birding optics for sale not far from Algona, Iowa, our destination. They were a famous name in binoculars and priced at something I could almost afford. I worked things out with my wife—"Poor Mrs. Batt," the neighbors call her—so that between the wedding and the reception I would drop her off at my aunt's place in Algona, and I would then venture out to have a look at the binoculars and return to pick my wife up in time for the reception. I had thought that once I had become a married man that my dancing days were over. My wife convinced me that was an erroneous assumption. I had to be at the reception to do a couple of slow dances and the chicken dance or the hokey-pokey.

Things went as planned. The couple was wed. I hit the groom in the ear with a glob of rice pudding. I dropped my wife at my aunt's and motored to the place offering the binoculars for sale. "Like new," read the ad in the newspaper. I imagined the birds I would be able to see with such fine glasses. The bins I had were too good for the likes of me, but were so cheap that the company that had manufactured them had refused to put its name on them. When people asked me what kind of binoculars I was using, I answered honestly that I didn't know. The ad had given directions to the farm, and I found it without any problem. I drove down the long driveway leading to the house. The drive was lined with pieces of machinery in various states of disrepair. They loomed ominously near the drive as if they were some prehistoric creatures. In the midst of the rusting hulks were a number of dogs—all looking mean and not a bit trustworthy. They made me wish I were wearing a suit of armor with my necktie.

I parked my old car and got out of it with some trepidation, keeping an eye on the mangy canines eyeing me back. They barked and growled unkind things in my direction. I made it to the shadows of the old house with my limbs still intact. I knocked on the door and a large, unshaven man wearing a torn and stained T-shirt partially covered with a pair of bib overalls with only one strap fastened, opened the door.

"Yeah?" he grunted in not the friendliest manner as he eyed the suit at his door suspiciously.

I got the required mention of the weather out of the way. It was a beautiful day.

The man looked me up and down as if he were measuring me for a casket. His uneasiness was apparent and nearly matched mine.

"What day of the week is this?" he asked, while scratching himself briskly. He was a multi-tasker.

I told him it was a Saturday.

"It is, huh?" he replied, distrust creeping even deeper into his voice. "Are you a banker?" he asked. His dogs growled.

I replied that I wished that I were one.

"Been to a funeral?" he wondered aloud.

"No, thank goodness."

"Are you a lawyer, then?" was the man's next question.

I assured him that I was not and put a hand in my own pocket as proof that I was not an attorney.

"Don't tell me you're the new minister? My wife said you might be stopping out. I've been meaning to get to church, but I was out of town, then I came down with that flu that has been going around. I hope you don't catch it. I just couldn't shake it and I've been awful busy. I promise that I'll try to make it next Sunday or maybe the Sunday after next. You can count on me being there at Christmas."

I told him that I was not the new minister.

"Then how come you're wearing a suit on a Saturday?" asked the big man in the bad overalls.

I looked the man squarely in the eye and said, "It's not every day that a man buys used binoculars."

Back to the Basics

It was one of those days that was all that it was cracked up to be. One of the field trips I lead regularly is for preschoolers. This day, I would be leading 18 kids and 7 adults on a trail along a lake. I had my binoculars and the kids had theirs. The kids were sporting discount binoculars. They were made by taping two tubes from rolls of toilet paper together, and then festooning them with bird and butterfly stickers. They were the best binoculars I have ever used for close focusing. String was taped to them for use as neck strap. My binoculars were lacking both tape and stickers, but were equipped with glass. We had a delightful walk. The kids were great, as were the birds. My charges marveled at the tree swallows going in and out of the bluebird boxes. They giggled at the antics of a very accommodating sora. Mudhens, ducks, and geese delighted them. In turn, the children delighted me. I smiled at the realization of the rewards I receive from the simple task of showing a bird to a child. I let the kids look through my binoculars. They saw a lot. They let me look through their binoculars. I saw everything.

Starlings

I dreamed I was a starling.

That's what has become of me. I used to dream about chasing my wife around and now I dream that I am an unpopular bird. Some might say that the starling is the poison ivy of birds.

I think the constant litany of political ads has warped my feeble brain.

A person who studies dreams—I think that professional field is known as "people who study dreams"—once told me that if I dream that I am a bird it means I will likely have Raisin Bran for breakfast the next morning. Wait, there's more. She said that I would have milk on it. I haven't encountered anything so uncanny since they took the bathroom out of the old schoolhouse.

I once wanted to be a woodpecker. My mother said that I could be anything I wanted to be. I decided a woodpecker was a noble profession, but I found flying difficult and the hammering on trees gave me a headache and a bloody nose. I shelved my dream of woodpeckerly fame.

Becoming a starling would be easier. Starlings do a cool wolf whistle. I'd be able to whistle at other women and my bride wouldn't be able to be mad at me because I was a mere bird.

Mozart liked starlings. Much of our music today can place its origin on the music produced by Wolfgang Amadeus Mozart. His friends probably called him Wolfie and he likely shared a love of the wolf whistle with his pet starling. When his starling died, a funeral was held and Mozart wrote a musical piece for the sad occasion.

Shakespeare wrote about starlings and their ability to talk in one of his plays. I think Shakespeare had a starling bobblehead, but I haven't been able to find any proof.

The starling is not so loved here as it was during the times of Mozart and Shakespeare. The bird has nearly as many bad habits as I do. I don't condemn the bird. I believe that everything is put here on Earth for a reason—everything except chiggers.

The starling came to this country because of Shakespeare. A rich pharmaceuticals manufacturer—pardon the redundancy—thought the USA should have the benefit of each of the birds mentioned by the Bard of Avon. On March 16, 1890—I remember the date because March 16 is my birthday; I was very young at the time of the release—the well-meaning Shakespearean scholar released a flock of starlings in Central Park in New York City.

The starlings immediately mugged the man, and with the money they took from him they bought up the best trees in Central Park—the trees with nest cavities overlooking panhandling pigeons—and promptly evicted the red-headed woodpeckers from their homes.

By 1949, starlings were in Alaska, albeit with a slightly different plumage—one with a parka.

Starlings are gluttons on the suet feeders and mobsters when it comes to nest cavities—you either pay protection or something bad could happen to you.

I asked my much better half (Poor Mrs. Batt) if she thought it was a good idea for me to become a starling.

My wife told me that the starling reminds her of every jerk she ever knew in high school, wrapped in feathers.

"You know, like you were," she added.

I'm going to make a good starling. Look for me in all the better field guides.

The Alarm Clock

My wife and I wake early.

We are early-risers.

It's not completely our idea.

A flicker discovered that the TV antenna on the roof of our house, just above our bedroom, makes for a wonderful drumming spot for him to proclaim his territory.

The bird's hammerings send vibrations throughout the house and throughout our dreams.

It's a most effective alarm clock.

The only sound that awakens me more quickly is the sound of the cat threatening to throw up.

Field Guides

A man stopped at the State Fair booth to ask me a question about a bird he had seen. I gave my opinion as to what I suspected the bird to be. In order to help with the identification, I showed the man its image in the *Sibley Guide to Birds*. It showed the species in various ages and plumages. I asked the man if his mystery bird was the one looking back at him from the page in the field guide.

"I can't say for sure," he replied. "The bird I saw was facing the opposite direction from the birds in the book."

Field Trips

I was leading some nice folks from Texas around, showing them the natural delights of Minnesota. They began to rib me on how everything in Texas was much bigger than what we were seeing in Minnesota. I spotted some painted turtles sunning themselves on a log protruding from a lake.

"Do you see those? Do you know what they are?" I asked.

"They look like turtles," came the answer.

"They may look like turtles," I said, "but they are Minnesota wood ticks."

Hoodie Hoo

On February 20, at noon, my wife and I ran outside (it was well below zero), waved our hands over our heads, and shouted, "Hoodie Hoo!" This is what scares winter away. If we didn't do this, winter would never leave.

I was wearing flip-flops. This is not a requirement, but I like to be comfortable while I "Hoodie Hoo." I am not normal and have no hopes or desires to ever be so.

Doing the "Hoodie Hoo" has worked every year. Winter has always ended.

It was Love at First Whiff

He asked me how he would know when he met the right woman.

I told him that he would know when he took her to a sewage pond to bird.

If, after that experience, she still asks him to call her—well, she might just be the one.

It's Not that Easy

I was leading a bird walk on a beautiful spring day. One of those spring days that songs are written about.

As the group stopped to marvel at the beauty of a tiny warbler, a bicyclist stopped. He asked some questions about birding. I answered his questions with a smile.

As he was about to leave, I felt the need to tell him that birding was harder than it looked.

I'll never forget his reply: "It would have to be."

My Father-In-Law's Hummingbirds

Flowers are gifts that continue to bring us happiness and memories long after they have left us.

Flowers also attract hummingbirds to our yards. A flower would earn its keep if it did nothing else.

Hummingbirds and butterflies have been described as flying flowers.

There is something about seeing hummingbirds coming to the sugar-water feeders that I put up each summer and fall. Don't get me wrong—I cherish the goldfinches clinging to the nyjer seed feeder and the mourning doves feeding on the ground under our feeding station. The inquisitive chickadees never fail to brighten my day. I enjoy the brashness and the blue of the blue jays. But there is something about the hummingbirds. Maybe it is the distance they migrate, flying more than 500 miles across the Gulf of Mexico. This is a remarkable feat by a bird that weighs no more than a quarter.

We are getting the last taste of summer in Minnesota. It is the weather that tells us this, not the calendar. The nights are growing cool and the weather reports are autumn-like. I watch a hummingbird feed on the sweet water. He has declared the feeder to be his territory and spends his day chasing any intruders away. Even with his testy personality, I cannot help but like him. One day, I will awaken and the seasons will have changed and my hummingbird will be gone.

My father-in-law and I shared a love for hummingbirds. He put up a number of feeders and rejoiced when the birds arrived. My father-in-law was a retired farmer and an ex-Marine, although "ex-" probably is not correct—I have found that "once a Marine, always a Marine."

The ancient Aztecs believed in reincarnation. They believed that hummingbirds were so courageous that only the bravest of warriors had a chance of coming back as a hummingbird. Maybe that's why my father-in-law liked hummingbirds—they could have been Marines, too.

I remember the day well. I was hosting a natural history cruise on a tour boat as it cruised on a beautiful lake in southern Minnesota. In the midst of the cruise, I spotted Mayo One, a helicopter/ambulance based out of Rochester, Minnesota. I made mention to the boat's passengers of the fine service the helicopter provides, how it gets to Rochester quickly from our location and how fortunate we are to have such a thing in the area. I also talked of how I can never see the flying ambulance without experiencing a touch of sadness and a feeling of emptiness in the pit of my stomach, knowing that the life of someone and the lives of his loved ones would be changed dramatically.

Little did I know that the patient who was a passenger on that helicopter was my father-in-law.

Fall comes too soon. I don't want summer to end. I want to feel the warmth in my bones and the soft breezes on my skin. I want to smell the sun shining on mowed hay. I want to continue to hear the sounds of summer—the morning chorus of birds and the cicada choir practice. At this time of year I don't remember the nearly unbearable heat and humidity or the bloodthirsty mosquitoes of summer. I remember the rains—not the heavy ones, but the gentle and polite ones. I forget the weeds and remember the flowers.

I watch my hummingbird guarding his food supply and I think of my father-in-law's fight for his life.

"Please stay," I say silently to the hummingbird buzzing around the feeder. "Please stay with me a little longer. Don't leave yet. I haven't known you long enough."

I remember saying the very same things to my father-in-law as he lay in that hospital bed fighting for his life. He lived through Iwo Jima and the raising of four teenagers, but his heart had worn out. My wonderful father-in-law has been gone for some time now. The hummingbird's visits are delightful reminders of his goodness.

"Please linger. Allow me to hold fast to your presence through fall and into the winter."

Summer leaves well before it has worn out its welcome. So do hummingbirds and fathers-in-law.

"Please let me remember the songs of your birds when the snow covers the ground."

The Governor's Visit

It wasn't the best of times, but it could have been a heck of lot worse.

It wasn't the worst of times; we were getting by.

The Hartland Loafers' Club (HLC) was meeting at Tweeten's in Hartland. Tweeten's was one of those small-town places where the elite met to drink coffee and discover what the rest of the world was up to. The members of the HLC did nothing during the meetings, talked about how they could do even less, and then went home to rest. All the world's problems were solved before a cup of coffee was consumed.

This would prove to be one of those days that would keep the HLC meeting even though it accomplishes nothing more than a case of coffee nerves.

The regulars were all there—cleverly spaced to avoid attention. The door to the convenience store that called itself Tweeten's opened. In came two men dressed in dark suits and sporting aviator style sunglasses that allowed them to see out and prevented anyone from seeing in. You could tell that these guys had some secrets. The two men took up their stations, one on each side of the door. It looked like a raid, but unless coffee beans were illegal, there was no reason to raid Tweeten's. It might have been a takeover attempt by the Norwegian Mafia, but that was quickly ruled out, as the men's clothes were color-coordinated. Thoughts of making a run for it danced through the members' heads. Just before panic set in, he came through the door. He was a large man with a bald head encircled by a strap holding Swarovski binoculars.

"Where's your bathroom?" he asked in a gravelly voice familiar to every Minnesota resident. It was Jesse Ventura, former pro wrestler and the governor of the Gopher State—our governor who could beat up your governor.

He was in the area to take part in the State Birding Opener. Opening day ceremonies took place at the Hartland Sewage Ponds. You could practically smell the birds from Tweeten's. Despite his conspiracy theories about the Minnesota Ornithologists' Union's State Records Committee and their concerted effort to deny his sighting of a crimson-collared grosbeak at Men's Wearhouse, Jesse was there to throw out the first gull.

The esteemed members of the fabled HLC watched as the governor made his way to the bathroom. His associates—bodyguards or whatever they were—moved to new stations, one on each side of the bathroom door. Maybe they were bathroom monitors? The HLC members watched silently because no one could think of anything appropriate to say. This was quite an honor for a small town like Hartland—302 people, four last names. The silence was deafening. The governor came out and left the store without another word. One HLC member was shocked that he would use a restroom without buying anything. Such behavior is just not Minnesotan. Another member wondered aloud if the governor had washed his hands. Some thought that they had heard water run in the sink, but nobody could be sure. Another opined that sometimes people run water just to make others think they washed their hands even when they didn't. This was a red-letter day for the Hartland Loafers Club. They had a story to tell that required no enhancing.

Things haven't been the same since that day. Jesse is no longer governor. Rather than depending upon memories to recollect the event, the HLC decided to put up a plaque commemorating this historic event. A committee was formed to look into forming a committee to appoint a committee dedicated to placing this plaque in a prominent position in Tweeten's.

It's a slow process. No one knows for sure what the governor did while he was in the bathroom. Therefore, no one has any idea what the plaque should say.

An Episode with a Pepper

I remember the day that I learned of the treachery of things that are disguised as food.

I was in Anzalduas County Park nestled along the Rio Grande near Mission, Texas. It was a beautiful Sunday afternoon and I was having a swell time looking at birds in the park. I had seen a clay-colored robin, a vermilion flycatcher, a northern beardless-tyrannulet, and a gray hawk. I was searching the trees for a tropical parula. The park was filled with people cooking and eating. The sun was shining and kids were playing. I was looking through my binoculars into the leaves of a giant tree, when I first heard the voice.

"What are you looking at?"

I turned to the questioner, a man, and told him that I was looking for a bird.

"Yeah?" he acknowledged. "I suppose that I'm getting to the age where I should start watching birds."

"Everyone should watch the birds. So, of course, you should start watching birds," I replied. "How old are you?"

He told me. He was the same age as I was. I asked him when his birthday was.

"March 16," he said.

"March 16? That's my birthday!" I said. Talk about your coincidences.

The next thing I knew, we were getting out our driver's licenses and showing them to one another. It was true. We were born on exactly the same day, with him being about an hour older than I am.

"It's a sign," he said. "Come on, you're coming over here and eating with my family."

I took him up on his offer. A man has to respect his elders—even if they are only so by about an hour. Besides, it fit into my three keys to happiness: never miss a chance to put your feet up, never miss the opportunity to go to the bathroom, and never pass up free food. I walked across the park to the picnic table where I was introduced to his family. My new friend, an electrician, had a wife and a 10-year-old daughter. They were charming and gracious hosts. I ate fried bread and beefsteak. The food was great. Then my host offered me a tiny bit of a concoction made from peppers.

"What is this?" I asked capturing a bit of pepper on my spoon.

Peppers worry me. I'm not good with friendly fire. I grew up in a Midwestern family where ketchup was considered an extremely hot seasoning. We used only three spices—salt, pepper, and ketchup. Even mustard was too exotic for us. We thought that peppers came in three forms—too hot, even hotter, and call the ambulance. My favorite song is, "There Ain't No Burrito Mild Enough."

"It's a habanero," he said with a smile.

"It's going to be very hot, isn't it?" I asked.

"No," he said with another smile. "It's like candy. Besides, the cracker will dominate the flavor." Men lie about such things. "Eat it. It's good for you. It will put hair on your chest."

I have hair on my chest. A man who owns a shirt only needs so much hair on his chest. I owned a shirt. I asked the same question of his wife. Women tell the truth about such things.

"It is very hot," she said. She gave me a sympathetic look. Perking up, she added, "It will certainly curl the hair you do have on your chest."

That was all I needed to hear to convince me not to eat the habanero pepper dish offered to me. Then I noticed the 10-year-old daughter looking at me. She was sizing me up. She was looking at me to see if I'd be man enough to eat the peppers. My manhood was at stake.

There was only one thing I could do.

I took a spoonful of the pepper mixture and tossed it into my mouth. I should have used a smaller spoon.

It was a hot day out. It became hotter in.

Fire in the hole! My car alarm went off.

How can I describe the sensation? It wasn't food; it was

a toxic waste spill. It was lip remover in a bowl. It was as painful as stepping on a Lego while barefoot in the middle of the night. My mouth was on fire. It was as if I were eating a dish of red-hot needles. I quickly realized that I had just taken a lifetime supply of the pepper. I wanted to wash it down with something cooler—like molten lava. Things got even worse. I had no milk to put out the dancing flames. Only dairy products are effective in putting out a pepper fire in my mouth. It burned my lip and it burned my tongue. It burned all the way to my stomach. I walked through five states before the fire went out. It was the ultimate diet food, but in just a couple of weeks, I was hungry again. I had eaten the habanero pepper soup of death and lived to tell the story.

My new friend called the concoction a double-burner. That meant it burned coming and going.

I have discovered that time does indeed heal all wounds. There are days now when my digestive system barely smolders.

I continue to enjoy birding in the Rio Grande Valley. My eyes have feasted on the sights of green kingfishers, blue mockingbirds, green jays, and crimson-collared grosbeaks. I have eaten many foods that were not a part of the fare on my childhood table. The peppers are hot, but the birds are cool.

Trout Day

It was my great pleasure to speak at Trout Day at Forestville State Park. It was a wonderful day with countless children enjoying a time outdoors on the Root River. The visit gave me the chance to pick bluebells with my eyes. The lovely flowers gracing the wooded edge were beyond beautiful. I gazed at the plants while being serenaded by a field sparrow singing from, where else, a field. The bird's whistled notes are repeated until they increase into a trill. It reminds me of a ping-pong ball bouncing upon a table. I left only tracks and took only memories at Forestville. It was a good exchange.

Memorial Day

I left the house on Memorial Day as a great crested flycatcher battled with its image in a window of our home.

I traveled to Flandreau State Park in New Ulm to meet with family members.

It was muggier than a root beer stand, so we headed to the swimming pool at the park. The beach was littered with folks.

I don't do well at beaches. Oh, I'm good at sitting on one of those bag chairs and reading a book. The problem is when I look up. I have to look somewhere and wherever I look at a beach, there is a fetching female that I shouldn't be looking at while sitting near my lovely wife. I shouldn't even be looking at them when not seated next to my bride. Either I need blinders or those dark sunglasses that show no hint of eyes that are favored by government agents that no one ever wants to meet. It didn't help that I had binoculars around my neck. Sitting on the small beach with the binoculars around my neck made me look even creepier than I really am. So I went for a walk.

The gnats were less than helpful. I hate to gnatpick, but they were so numerous that I had to fall back on my usual defensive technique. I swallowed as many as I could.

I climbed a trail to a spot where I heard racking coughs. There I surprised three young lads not enjoying their first Marlboros.

Then the birds took over.

I listened to the *sweet, sweet, sweet, I'm so sweet* song of the yellow warbler. The voice of the summer warbler.

I listened to the wood thrush advertising salty snacks with its ethereal, flutelike *Frito Lay* song.

I saw a lovely scarlet tanager (a black-winged redbird) and watched a yellow-billed cuckoo devour caterpillars with gusto.

As I walked back to the family gathering, a red admiral butterfly landed on my shoulder. That meant either good luck or it had mistaken me for a bird dropping.

Either way was OK with me. I'd been birding. I'd already been lucky.

Eurasian Collared-Dove

I pulled my Pontiac off the highway into Hinton, Iowa. I was searching for a park. My wife had made sandwiches and placed them into a soft-sided cooler. I wanted a spot to sit and enjoy the April sun.

I found a location, parked the car, and we began to eat.

Then I heard the call. It wasn't the *hula-hoop-hoop-hoop* of the mourning dove. It was a three-note song: *koo-KOO-kook*. I had heard the sound before. It's made by the Eurasian collared-dove that was introduced into the Bahamas in the 1970s. Some migrated to Florida in the 1980s. It wasn't long before the doves found their way to exotic places like Minnesota and Iowa.

The Eurasian collared-dove has a black collar on its nape. It is larger, chunkier, and paler than the mourning dove, which lacks the black collar. Its blunt-tipped tail is fan-shaped when spread. The mourning dove's tail is longer and pointed.

It provided another reason for dining outdoors. If we'd been eating indoors, we'd have missed a cool experience.

It was a life bird like every bird I see or hear. It wasn't a bird that I'd not seen before, but a bird that made life more interesting.

The Cell Phone Chronicles

I needed to make a phone call, but my cell phone works indoors only on beautiful days. On blustery days that even Pollyanna would describe as miserable, I need to go outside to use the cell phone.

Grumbling to myself, I stumbled out into the wind and rain.

Before I was able to place my call, I heard the sound of a sandhill crane. The big bird bugling as it flew overhead brought me a joy that I shared in my subsequent phone conversation.

A crane, standing guard, was once believed to hold a stone in its foot to keep it awake. Some cultures believed that the souls of the dead rode to heaven on the backs of cranes.

Now whenever my cell phone refuses to work indoors, I consider it a wonderful excuse to go outdoors.

The Eye of a Storm

The year had hit us with hailstorms, tornadoes, and floods. Then it surprised us with a land hurricane. A plummeting barometric pressure led to winds stronger than those produced by campaigners for public office. The weather has become more alarming since we started speaking of weather events. I placed rocks in my pockets to keep from being blown away. The heavy winds caused my house to cry out in the night. I interpreted the sounds as my house calling, "Uncle! Uncle!"

As I drove down the road, the radio voice told me that there was an eye to the storm and it was located near Duluth. As I continued driving, I entered another kind of an eye. It was the eye of a blackbird storm. A flock of endless blackbirds surrounded my car. They swirled about me as if they were auditioning for roles in Hitchcock's movie, *The Birds*.

I watched the birds as they read the earth in a way I could only imagine. The birds were foraging, attempting to find a decent breakfast.

Something To Crow About

The sun promised a good day. I heard the crows talking in the treetops. They argued and laughed.

The morning was going as most do—much too quickly. I took a chicken from his roost and set him on the ground. He crows constantly from the beam he spends nights on. His crows are good but he ends them in a pitiful wheeze. I used a rake, placing it gently under him so that he would step on it. It was an elevator to the ground floor for this less-than-nimble rooster. Sometimes the process was like turning a cruise ship around as the loosely put-together bird stumbled over the lawn implement. On the ground, he clucked his appreciation at my small kindness. It's a lot to go through for a rooster, but I don't mind. Folks say, "It's just a chicken."

I don't think any creature is a "just a." Helping the rooster gave my day an ordinary splendor.

Once the rooster's feet were firmly planted on *terra firma*, he began to make those odd sounds that indicated a flying predator was near. I told the rooster that it was just a crow or two, but he continued vocalizing. A red-tailed hawk flew overhead.

I said, "You were right."

The rooster looked at me and crowed—there was no trailing wheeze.

There was a Bluebird

It was a good time for bad weather.

It was March in Minnesota.

A storm dumped more than 20 inches of snow on what I call home.

The storm was reminiscent of the blizzards I experienced when I was a boy. March was like living in a snow globe in those days of yore.

This storm caused every hotel in the area to become filled. Those who could not find a hotel room found shelter in the National Guard Armory.

I joined the Shovel Olympics early in the morning after the storm had subsided. I shoveled with as much gusto as I could muster. I was outdoors and it was exercise. It was fun.

For a while.

The shovel became heavier with each scoop.

I soon grew weary of the chore and began dreaming of being marooned on Gilligan's Island with the fearless crew, the millionaire and his wife, the professor, Ginger, and Mary Ann. Especially with Ginger.

It was then that I saw it. It was a male eastern bluebird on a snow bank.

The blue of the bird highlighted against the white of the snow took my breath away.

Shoveling became easier.

We don't always get what we want. We are given what we need.

I needed to see a bluebird.

It was so good to see him.

Not all blessings are in disguise.

James Matthew Barrie wrote that we are given memories that we might have roses in December.

Perhaps I was given a glimpse of blue so that I might make it until the snow melted.

I saw the bluebird because I looked. Yogi Berra said, "You can see a lot just by observing."

I am a birder. For years, I have been unable to look friends in the eyes. Oh, I've tried, but my vision keeps shifting to a bird flying overhead. I drive my spousal unit crazy by identifying the birds calling during a romantic movie or telling her that some of the birds couldn't possibly be calling in the area where the film is supposedly taking place. I've watched televised golf just to hear the singing birds. I have changed the Man's Prayer from the *Red Green Show* to suit my purpose: "I'm a birder, but I can change, if I have to, I guess."

I loved seeing the bluebird and I wished him traveling mercies. Seeing the bluebird brought a song featuring bluebirds to my mind. There are many songs featuring this beautiful creature.

Although the song that occurred to me was a huge hit during World War II, *There'll Be Bluebirds Over The White Cliffs of Dover* was a fantasy. There are no bluebirds in Dover. Dover is in the county of Kent in England, and bluebirds are indigenous only to North America.

"There'll be bluebirds over the white cliffs of Dover.
Tomorrow, just you wait and see.
There'll be love and laughter and peace ever after,
Tomorrow, when the world is free.

The shepherd will tend his sheep,
The valley will bloom again,
And Jimmy will go to sleep,
In his own little room again.

There'll be bluebirds over the white cliffs of Dover.
Tomorrow, just you wait and see.
There'll be love and laughter and peace ever after,
Tomorrow, when the world is free."

I've always known that a bluebird is a symbol of happiness—even when it is not there.

It didn't bother me that the song was not factual. I was just happy that there are bluebirds where I am.

When my parents moved to Minnesota, they bought an old farmhouse with door locks that they never used. There was a key that would have locked and unlocked each of that old house's doors if my parents had chosen to use it. This key was called a skeleton key—it opened every door.

To me, a bluebird is like a skeleton key. If you want to see and enjoy nature, a bluebird will open the door for you.

They Called Him Red

It was early in the morning and I was working hard to resurrect my mailbox.

It had fallen prey to that dreaded predator, an over-zealous snowplow driver. A case of drive-by snowplowing. The flying mailbox gave an entirely new meaning to the term "airmail."

I had nearly completed my task when a friend drove up and got out of her vehicle. She carried a cardboard box that housed a tiny, red eastern screech-owl. The little owl, which certainly fit the description of cute, was unable to fly, which was why he showed up at the end of my driveway.

My wife and I have been hauling hawks, owls, eagles, and falcons to the Raptor Center located at the University of Minnesota for some years. The Raptor Center strives to restore injured birds of prey to good health and release them back into the wild whenever possible.

Because of an overly ambitious calendar, I would not be able to take the screech-owl to the Raptor Center until later that day.

Work reared its ugly head, and it was 8:00 at night by the

time our adventure began. I called the Raptor Center and was told that a volunteer would be waiting for me at the end of my journey of a couple of hours. Love makes the world go around, and volunteers do much of the spinning.

The weather was quite nice, but proved to be the lull between storms. I picked one of the worst nights for driving. The elements conspired against me, but I was resolute. The snow fell heavily at an angle dictated by a strong wind. There wasn't much traffic in the northbound lane of I-35—mostly tractor-trailer rigs shivering along at 40 mph and snowplows with so many flashing lights that I felt as though I were driving through a Bee Gees infested disco. Icy roads, strong winds, blowing snow, and the car radio's scariest of weather reports. I knew it would have been wise not to be on the road, but I was well into my journey when the nasty weather hit. There is no such thing as bad weather, just bad drivers and bad clothing. I needed to get to the owl hospital. I had a patient to think of.

We had a convoy—a line of big trucks and a man with a small owl. The owl wanted to turn around and go home, but I was steadfast. I replaced the radio's weather reports with a CD of the William Tell Overture—music made for driving in Minnesota winters. It strengthened our resolve. At least it strengthened mine. I cannot speak for the owl.

The weather improved with the miles. As I neared my destination, the weather had improved so much that it could be described as "horrific."

I was late getting there, but mission impossible had become mission accomplished. The owl was in the extremely capable hands of the good people at the Raptor Center.

As I drove home, I hoped and prayed for my friend, the little red screech-owl. Although the temperature continued to drop, I turned down the car's heater. I didn't need its hot air. I felt warm all over.

A Walkabout

I was walking down a trail not far from a large airport. It was a beautiful day made for a walk.

As I happily hoofed my way down the path, I ran into a face-high spider web.

It was a big one. I began to battle with the web by flailing away with my arms in that special martial arts that works only on spider webs.

After a time, I freed myself from the web. I looked across a meadow and saw a group of people sitting on a bench. They were staring at me. They couldn't see the spider web, but they had seen my odd actions.

I walked the trail leading away from them.

Winter Work

It feels like one of those days that used to be.

I am walking to the mailbox with my faithful canine companion, Towhee. We are on a mission. We are getting the mail. My dog has a boundless zest for these walks. It is one of the highlights of her day and I have nothing better to do.

We are walking to the mailbox, but my dog and I lose our way. We missed our turn.

It's Towhee's fault.

She finds dead things on our walks.

My dog's New Year's resolution is to smell even more like a dead squirrel. She likes to roll on dead things. Dogs have a perverted idea of what constitutes a roll-on deodorant.

A light snow had fallen during the night. I like snow. It softens the world. It deadens sounds and makes the landscape look fresh and new. The only things spoiling the pristine state of our yard are the footprints of earlier travelers. The dog and I both examine the tracks left in the snow by rabbits, squirrels, pheasants, and cats. Towhee has a conspiracy theory about each one. She gives each track a thorough snuffling.

The footprints thoroughly investigated, we move on.

The leaves hanging stubbornly onto a red oak tree clack in the breeze as we walk by. It's part of the winter symphony.

I stop to marvel at the beauty of the cardinals feeding on the ground and to listen to the whistling wings of a small flock of mourning doves escaping our presence. I have work to do, but it can wait. Work was invented for folks who don't like to look at birds.

I hear a whistle other than that of the wings of the doves.

Both the dog and I look up to see a red-tailed hawk flying overhead and making the whistling sound. The beautiful buteo is hunting.

We weren't the only ones to take notice of the raptor. The hawk whistled up a murder of crows. The crows quickly form a gang. The four corvids begin to caw and attack the hawk from above. They dive-bomb the hawk, making contact with their beaks. Towhee and I become mesmerized watching the feathered dogfight.

It's easy to see that the crows relish their work. If a bird could smile, the four large, black birds would be smiling. The crows continue the cacophony as they attempt to cuss the intruder from the area.

The dog and I watch as the drama in the skies takes place.

We watch for a long time, forgetting all other matters of the day.

After the combatants fly from our sight, the dog and I walk into the house.

"Hadn't the mail come yet?" asks my wife.

We had forgotten to get the mail.

The dog and I go outside again. She has a boundless

zest for these walks and I am determined to actually make it to the mailbox this time.

My Choice is the Chickadee

I was in school the other day, working off detention hours that had managed to accumulate with interest over the years.

I was talking to a third grade class. I like talking to kids. I can fool some of them into thinking that I'm a grown-up. They are more likely to believe my stories than, say, someone like—let's not mention any names here; let's just call her my wife. Kids are great. I think everyone should try to be one at some point in his or her life.

One of the boys in the class asked me what my favorite bird was. I told him that it was the black-capped chickadee. You should have seen his face. He looked like I had just told him that he'd be having spinach for dessert.

He said, "Chickadee? That's a wimpy bird to have as a favorite."

I knew where he was coming from, having once been a third grader myself. My family calls the third grade the best three years of my life. He was a third grader, which meant he liked hawks, owls, eagles, and falcons—the Terminators of the bird world. If Arnold Schwarzenegger, Bruce Willis, Russell Crowe, or Sylvester Stallone were birds, they would be raptors. I like all birds, but the chickadee is my main Avian American. Let me tell you why. Join me in my dream sequence. Some odd music will play as the picture blurs.

The thermometer in the yard near my home told me that the temperature was 20 degrees below zero. That meant it could be any month in Minnesota. It was so cold, that the guy selling me heating oil wasn't smiling. I wore all of the clothes I owned while I filled the bird feeders. A chickadee landed nearby and began to sing. He sang not of the miserable weather, but of the blue sky and the warm sun of tomorrow. The chickadee is the top salesman of the feathered crowd—energetic and enthusiastic. This cheerful little ball of feathers is about the size of a man's thumb. The song of this small bird made me forget the cold, the snow, the ice, and the wind. OK, I didn't forget the wind. The wind was blowing the whiskers off my face.

Curious and friendly, the chickadee brightened my day as not even the sun would have been able.

The black-capped chickadee has a black cap, a black bib, white cheeks, pale buff flanks, and a gray back. Its song is a *chick-a-dee-dee-dee* or a whistled *fee-bee*. The *fee-bee* has been described as "Love you," "Sweetie," or "Spring's here." The "Spring's here" call is given in winter, so the bird can be overly enthusiastic. Not a bad thing. I expect to see a chickadee selling something on one of those TV shopping channels any day.

Chickadees are regular visitors to feeders. Their favorite food is the sunflower seed and they are attracted to suet. A flock of chickadees has a definite pecking order with subordinate birds waiting until the dominant birds are through eating. This hyperactive little bird has a body temperature of 108 degrees, and to maintain that temperature the chickadee must eat like an NFL defensive tackle. The chickadee grabs a sunflower seed, flies to a tree limb, grasps the seed with a petite foot, and pecks vigorously to break the shell. It caches seeds in tree bark for consuming later. The bird is as happy eating upside-down as it is dining right-side-up. With a little effort, many people have trained chickadees to take food from a hand.

Chickadees form small flocks in early fall. The flock circulates around its territory, feeding in productive spots, and fighting small gang wars with neighboring flocks. Birders know that other birds travel with chickadees—downy woodpeckers, tufted titmice, white-breasted nuthatches, brown creepers, kinglets, and various species of warblers. Why do these other birds like to hang with the chickadees? Is it because the chickadees have season tickets to the Vikings? Possibly, but I don't think so. There are at least two reasons that chickadees make wonderful flying companions. Like truck drivers, the chickadees know all of the best places to eat. The second reason is that the chickadees have a great predator alarm system. The first chickadee to spot a predator gives a warning call. Something like Tonto did for The Lone Ranger all those years. It cries *chick-a-dee-dee-dee*—the more *dees*, the greater the threat. The flock responds to this warning by freezing in place. The other chickadees begin to utter thin notes while demonstrating a talent for ventriloquism. These disembodied calls coming from every direction tend to confuse predators. Once the intruder leaves, a chickadee sounds an "all's well" call and the flock returns to searching for food.

Chickadees make me smile even on days when my lips are frozen shut.

Memorial Day

It was my honor to give a Memorial Day address this year. Giving such a talk is always a humbling experience for me. As I remembered our heroes, I saw many chimney swifts fly over the park where I spoke. The band played and the swifts twittered. As I traveled about to graduation parties, chimney swifts seemed to be the bird that accompanied me. Eating lunch today in my favorite cafe, I tried to carry on a proper conversation with my dining companions, but my eyes constantly strayed to watch the chimney swifts flying above the eatery. Our lunch hour flew by. Time goes by swiftly, especially while watching swifts go by.

Raspberry Canes Ripped My Flesh

I carried a plastic jug that once held bottled water. Its handle was looped through the belt holding my trousers in place. I had cut a hole in the top of the bottle to make it easy to drop the raspberries into.

The heat was stifling, the brambles attacked me with the ferocity of bridesmaids after a bouquet, and the mosquitoes welcomed me with an unquenchable thirst for blood.

The birds complained. Thrasher, robin, catbird, and oriole encouraged me to shop elsewhere.

I was steadfast in my endeavor to accumulate as many black raspberries (blackcaps) as I could.

The next morning, I enjoyed raspberries covered in milk and sugar. It was sinfully good and it helped my wounds to heal.

Things I've Learned while Birding

It was the cerulean warbler of happiness.

Birders had gathered to enjoy the avian delight. Birding is a flame that is most treasured when shared. Most of the group expressed wonderment with occasional flashes of identification skills tossed in. I waited until the others had expressed themselves fully about the subject dancing in the treetops before uttering this line from Monty Python's *Dead Parrot Sketch*: "Remarkable bird, the Norwegian Blue, idnit, ay? Beautiful plumage."

A hush fell over the crowd. It was a small hush. No one was injured.

No one sought further comment from me. However, one did ask, "Has anyone ever told you that you are one of the world's greatest birders?"

"No," I said.

"Have you ever wondered why?"

I hadn't. I'm not a complete moron. I know stuff. I know the name of every bird in the world—as long as it's "Bob" and I know there are no experts, only students, in the crowd. I watch and I wonder. Abraham Heschel wrote, "The beginning of our happiness lies in the understanding that life without wonder is not worth living."

The Red Queen told Alice in *Through the Looking Glass*, "Here, you see, it takes all the running you can do to keep in the same place." The Red Queen could have been a birder. A birder needs to learn things constantly to replace the things forgotten. At least until all birds start wearing nametags and singing their names.

Once upon a time, we learned to tie our shoes, to spell our names, to do fractions, that McDonald's isn't the place to go for pizza, to use verbs, and that when the cashier says "Strip down" she's talking about a credit card. I'll never be allowed back into that store. At least, most of us learned those things. I had a few infractions while doing fractions. I think I got a third of them right, but I'm not sure.

"Pay attention," said my teacher. "One day, you'll find use for what I'm teaching you."

"Yeah, right," I thought. "When pigs fly."

It wasn't long before a flock of bacon oinked overhead.

I've learned things while making birding my default mode. Even though I walk through the valley of bird counts, I fear no evil for my binoculars are with me.

I've learned that looking at birds brings unexpected pleasures. I'm only as old as I look, so I'd better look. If I don't look, I don't see any birds. Birders are like bird feeders—they work best outdoors. That said, few things please me more than seeing familiar birds at my feeders.

I've learned that some birds are equipped with cloaking devices. The secret to finding a nemesis bird is to keep looking for it or to stop looking for it.

I've learned to curb the knock-knock jokes. Well, almost.

I say, "Knock-knock."

You say, "Who's there?" And you say it well.

I answer, "Consumption."

"Consumption, who?" You are good.

"Consumption be done about all these starlings?"

I've learned to hang on tightly to my teacup or a kind birder will fill it with coffee.

Seymour Berdz, who believes that his guess is always better than mine, claimed that he was abducted by aliens, taken into their spaceship where he was stripped and probed, wed to an extraterrestrial, and returned home in time to see an evening grosbeak. I couldn't believe it. I mean, come on, an evening grosbeak at that time of the year. I've learned that some guys should stick to decaf.

A birder evolves. There will always be mysteries. Blessings are disguised. I can't always hit a home run, but I can advance the runners by persistent learning.

I learned something the day I was vacuuming the sprinkles off a doughnut. Dieting is hard.

"Really? You're going to wear that shirt?" said my wife. She prefers that I wear something that matches her purse in case I need to hold it in the mall.

"It's my favorite shirt," I replied. It had some mileage on it.

"It's too bad it doesn't come in your size. It's covered in food stains. It looks like a buffet," spoke management.

"That's why it's my favorite," I said.

"I don't know how many times I've asked you to get rid of that shirt," my wife added, refusing to let it go.

"You should keep better records," I said, chortling with the knowledge that I'd saved "You aren't the boss of me" for another day.

Soon after that, my wife and I visited St. Olaf Cemetery. I was wearing a different shirt—a clean one.

We weren't there because we had a coupon. We were there to water the plants adorning the graves of loved ones.

A cemetery is a peaceful place, safer than home. Many people are injured in their homes, but not many are injured in cemeteries. A cemetery is a great place to seek the company of birds. A cemetery is the perfect place to try to remember what I was worried about a year ago.

As we strolled about the cemetery after completing our tasks, we stopped to pay our respects to those we knew and those we didn't. Some had lived to a grand old age, but most had died too young. Not all were carried gently to their final resting places. Most of the deceased hadn't eaten enough beets, spinach, or other things they didn't like. I was looking for an epitaph reading "It's just a pulled muscle" when my wife pointed to a tombstone and said, "Do not get me a monument like that one."

I hadn't thought about buying her a grave marker.

I hadn't thought about many things. That was just one of them. When my wife asks, "Honey, what are you thinking about?" and I answer "Nothing," she believes me.

I knew why she didn't want one like it. The gravestone was covered with bird poop. Either the birds found it a comforting place to relieve themselves, or it scared the crap out of them. It wasn't the grave of a fellow named John Privy, so perhaps it was the stone's color, size, shape, or location that attracted them.

I was surprised by my wife's comment about buying a headstone. Like most husbands, I figure I'll be the first to shuffle off this mortal coil.

It's not a pleasant thought, but quietus is like the objects in the mirror that are closer than they appear. Life's odometer turns quickly. Everyone has an expiration date.

If she goes first, my wife's epitaph will read, "No pooping on this gravestone!"

I'm betting she will outlive me.

Chapter 3:
Capers Close to Home

Feeding the Koi

A friend has koi in his backyard pond.

As near as I can figure it, koi is a refined goldfish. I'm guessing this fish has a little more education and is certainly better mannered than the loutish, run-of-the-mill goldfish.

My friend enjoys his koi. He feeds them Cheerios. The koi love the wily breakfast cereal.

Once upon a time, I watched a beautiful male cardinal feed sunflower seeds to koi. The redbird would grab a sunflower seed from the feeder and fly down to the pond's edge. A koi would come to the surface and make that, well, er, uh, fish mouth. The cardinal would feed it.

When a cardinal sees a mouth, it wants to put food in it. My mother had the same inclination whenever we had company.

The cardinal feeds the koi because he thinks they need feeding.

The cardinal does this because he has very strong parental instincts.

Or maybe cardinals just like koi.

Mister Rogers

A young red-tailed hawk hangs around my neighborhood. I call him Mister Rogers. It's his neighborhood.

Gray partridges live here, too. When the snow gets deep, the partridges and pheasants come to eat under our feeders. They don't want to be there. The lack of food and habitat force them to feed at our trough.

I like watching them.

So does Mister Rogers.

One day, Mister Rogers made his move.

He attempted to take a partridge out for lunch.

He missed.

The partridge flew into some shrubs—a thicket, with bramble leanings. There was no pear tree available.

The hawk flew into a tree just above the location of the partridges.

A male partridge began to scold the hawk. He did so from the safety of his hiding place deep in the thicket.

I don't speak fluent partridge, but I don't believe that what he was saying was in any way complimentary towards the hawk.

The hawk took umbrage.

He made a number attempts to get to his dinner on wings.

Each time he tried, he found himself getting his wings tangled in the thicket.

Finally, the raptor gave up.

For the partridge, it was a beautiful day in the neighborhood.

Barred Owls

I heard a barred owl call recently. It called, *Who cooks for you? Who cooks for you all?* It followed this familiar vocalization with maniacal laughter. It ended its diurnal performance with a *hoo-wah* that I am sure Al Pacino used in the movie *Scent of a Woman*.

The barred owl is beautiful. It produces such a wide

selection of sounds that one writer described it as "date night at the insane asylum."

The Catbird's Song

The resident catbird in our yard begins to sing as early as two o'clock in the morning. The catbird is a mimic and its song is a long, slow series of warbled notes, ranging from whistles to squeaks, often including imitations of the songs and calls of other birds. The catbird's song is a jumble of disjointed notes. If you listen long enough, somewhere in that mixture of notes you will hear the bird's trademark *meow* call that gives the bird its ironic name. The notes are not repeated twice as in the song of the brown thrasher. The catbird offers no apology for its discordant song. As the good book says, "make a joyful noise" and the catbird does that.

A catbird is a sleek bird, not much larger than an oriole. The gray catbird is gray except for a black cap and a chestnut patch under the base of the tail. The male and female are identical in plumage. There is an old poem titled "The Catbird's Song," written by John G. Ellenbecker that reads:

>Don't you hear the catbird singing / In the cedar tree? /
>Oh how must his heart be swinging /
>In that merry glee!
>*Parka, parka, tuleree, tuleree, chrup, cheerup*—
>How he loves that song!
>*Wet-year, wet-year, terry, terry, hark, hark*—
>What a liquid throng!
>From early morn till dark he chatters, /
>Happy as a king; / Sending forth his brook of laughter /
>From his choral spring.
>*Parka, parka, tuleree, tuleree, chrup, cheerup*—
>What a babbling poet!

Wet-year, wet-year, terry, terry, hark, hark—
Does he really know it?"

The catbird singing in my yard has given my alarm clock some time off.

Fore!

I was visiting a friend's place. We were out in her yard, using binoculars to look up into a spruce tree. We were admiring the beautiful white-winged crossbills that were working the tree. The birds' bills are adapted for removing seeds from cones, starting at the bottom of a cone and spiraling upward, prying open each scale and removing the seeds with their tongues. We stopped staring upward to allow our necks to unkink, when a spruce cone came tumbling down and hit me on top of my head.

"Ouch!" I said.

My friend added, "That was no accident."

Cowbird Chronicles

I saw a chipping sparrow feeding a young brown-headed cowbird. The baby was much bigger than the adult.

Cowbirds lay their eggs in the nests of other birds and depend upon the foster parents to raise their progeny. Some do, some don't. Certain bird species chuck the eggs out of the nest. Other bird species build a new nest on top of the old one containing the cowbird egg. The surviving cowbirds mature and fly off to join their kindred.

Cowbirds do not ask for volunteers to accept an egg. Chipping sparrows are one of the birds whose nests are often parasitized by cowbirds.

To the tiny sparrow, feeding the large cowbird, it must be like filling the tank of a gas-guzzling, Rhode Islandsized SUV while employed at a minimum wage job.

The sparrow has a strong parental instinct. Many birds are wired to provide a gaping mouth with food. I have witnessed cardinals feeding koi at the edge of a pond.

As I watched the big baby cowbird ravenously taking food from the beak of a surrogate mother half its size, I was reminded of something my mother once said to me.

She told me that a mother loves her babies no matter what they become.

I guess that is true about birds, too.

A Red Raven

I enjoyed reading the works of Edgar Allen Poe.

"Enjoyed" might not be the right word. Poe scared the dickens out of the boyhood me. There weren't enough oats in the world to feed all the nightmares I had after reading Poe.

Poe wrote in his famous piece of literature, "The Raven:"

> "Once upon a midnight dreary, while I pondered weak and weary,
> Over many a quaint and curious volume of forgotten lore,
> While I nodded, nearly napping, suddenly there came a tapping,
> As of someone gently rapping, rapping at my chamber door.
> "Tis some visitor,' I muttered, tapping at my chamber door—
> Only this, and nothing more."

Later Poe introduced the visitor:

> "Open here I flung the shutter, when, with many a flirt and flutter,
> In there stepped a stately raven of the saintly days

of yore.
Not the least obeisance made he; not a minute
stopped or stayed he;
But, with mien of lord or lady, perched above my
chamber door—
Perched upon a bust of Pallas just above my
chamber door—
Perched, and sat, and nothing more."

One afternoon, while I pondered weak and weary, while I nodded nearly napping, suddenly there came a tapping, as of someone gently rapping, rapping at my window.

I thought of Poe's raven, while I did a CSI Minnesota. That investigation revealed that my tapping rapper was a beautiful male cardinal. A small bird hitting the window in a big way. Robins, orioles, chipping sparrows, and great crested flycatchers are other birds that have assaulted my windows. A bluebird took a few shots at his reflected image one day. A friend had a wild turkey doing battle with his reflection in a basement window.

The cardinal flung itself against the window as if he were wanted in five states. This action delighted our two housecats, Ethel and Purl. Our cats are the definition of housecats. They don't set a paw outdoors. The cats' analyst tells me that Ethel and Purl are as normal as anyone who lives with me could be expected to be. I digress.

The redbird battered my window because he had issues. Birds fight with their images in windows because their brains aren't sending a memo saying, "Stop it! That's you!" They are fighting with themselves. Before you think that's strange, realize that we fight with ourselves each day. The "Should I have a piece of pie or should I stick with my diet" conflict is fought daily in finer restaurants nationwide.

Birds believe the mirrored images to be a threat to territory and battle them with a fury. The battles are usually waged by males—that's how we roll—but females will join the fray.

I calmly asked the cardinal, "Why can't we all just get along?"

The skirmish continued, because a bird's image in a mirror is not easily intimidated. Most attacks last no more than a few days; some are triggered during periods of the day when the light is just right to produce a reflection. Some birds stretch the combat out for weeks.

The birds dirty windows—leaving prints of bills and wings. A window waits in hope that one day its prints will come.

Sometimes the attacking birds act as feathered alarm clocks, saving a homeowner money. When a bird wakes you, you can unplug the clock radio and save on the electric bill.

Should I have enrolled the cardinal in an anger management class? Should I have attempted to break up the image of his perceived foe in the glass? I could have done that by soaping the outside of the window, but my artistic pattern would have tipped off the neighbors as to who had been soaping their windows each Halloween. I could have put cardboard over the outside of the glass and listened for Martha Stewart's shudder. I could have placed a screen or plastic wrap held in place over the glass by duct tape—my favorite home repair tool. It's important to cover the outside of the window. Pulling the drapes or closing the blinds would likely enhance the mirrored image.

Plastic owls are marketed to discourage bird activity. Birds may not be able to discern themselves in a mirror but they quickly figure out that a plastic owl is a threat only to plastic birds.

I opted for patience. The cardinal's wrath subsided.

Poe wrote, "Quoth the raven, 'Nevermore.'"

My cardinal said to the window, "Nevermore" and got on with his life.

Poe had his rapping raven. I had mine.

Mine was red.

Birding the Backyard

Chimney swifts, looking like flying cigars, fed on air-borne insects. The swifts live up to their name and nest in chimneys. Indigo buntings sang, *Fire, fire. Where, where? Here, here. Put-it-out, put-it-out.* Barn swallows lined the utility wires before my presence caused them to take flight. They sliced through the air above me, calling *switch-it.* They had begun staging for a journey to Central or South America. I watched an oriole, knowing that I might not see many of them until next spring. Young rose-breasted grosbeaks, thick-billed and brownish, frequented the feeders, the females showing yellow under their wings and the males flashing red under theirs, about to embark on their first migration south. I will miss them and their sweet-tongued parents whose whistled songs enthralled me. Common nighthawks flew overhead, their white wing patches making them look like bats with headlights. These birds are leaving me. They need to be places where I am not. I'll miss the migrating birds. I am given sweet corn to lessen my loss.

In a Bit of a Jam

The day started as most of my days do.

I was sitting in a chair, silently chanting, "I don't want to be a grown-up. I don't want to be a grown-up," when my

A LIFE GONE TO THE BIRDS

wife interrupted my daily routine by calling me to the large window in our living room.

"That oriole has been in our jelly feeder for a long time. I wonder if he is okay?" she said.

I looked where she pointed. I always do. I am a dutiful husband. I saw the feeder I had rigged up to hold a small plastic dish filled with grape jelly. Orioles stopped by regularly to sample the grape. I could see that there was a male Baltimore oriole in the feeder. He appeared alert, but he wasn't doing much moving. I worried that he might have been injured.

I told my wife that I would investigate. She agreed to wait by the window and wring her hands in a motherly fashion.

Out the door I went. I walked to the feeder. The oriole saw me and scrunched down, peering over the top of the feeder.

I walked closer. The oriole played peek-a-boo with me. I touched the feeder. The oriole opened his bill in an avian martial arts pose.

I saw why he hadn't flown. He was stuck in the gooey grape jelly. I had fed jelly to orioles for many years and this guy was the first one ever caught in it. I assumed that he was nowhere near the top of his graduating class.

I attempted to free the oriole from the sucking goo. I was careful not to hurt the bird while he in turn busied himself by chewing on that sensitive web of skin that stretches between my thumb and index finger. I was able to extricate the oriole from the jelly with the loss of only several small feathers—all his. The question was, what do I do with an oriole that thought he was a jelly sandwich?

My sticky friend and I entered the house and were met by my wife who ordered a bath for our guest. You know mothers—that's their answer for everything. Into the bathroom we marched. I released the loose grip I had on the oriole and was surprised that he didn't stick to my hand. He climbed onto my finger and began to preen. My wife said that she knew it would be a male because a female would have known better than to get herself into such a sticky situation. The bird and I gave each other the look—the look that husbands have been giving each other forever.

I gave the oriole a gentle bath using lukewarm water and patted him dry with a towel that said "HERS" on it. By the time I had given him a second bath, the bird and I had become friends. You give someone a couple of baths and you bond. I washed and dried while the bird preened.

After we had finished his third bath, the oriole started making little happy sounds. The sounds stopped when he made an important discovery in the bathroom mirror. He froze before cocking his head in an attempt to get a better look at this punk oriole with the spiked feathers. He uttered what I believed to have been threats of bodily harm toward the intruder in the mirror. I held my buddy close to the scruffy looking bird in the mirror. My friend, who obviously felt he could easily handle the loser he saw in front of him, took a shot. He gave the mirror a hearty peck. That was enough.

First this sticky food all over him, and now he runs into Superoriole, the bird of steel.

I continued to give the bird baths; he continued to preen while giving the dirtiest looks he dared to his image in the mirror. He was willing to taunt and threaten his rival, but whenever I moved him close to the mirror, the oriole took a hike from my finger to my elbow.

After a dozen baths and a like number of dryings, the oriole was looking good. He began to sing—a beautiful whistle. My wife gave him a lecture about the sticky qualities of jelly and informed him that there was no need for anyone to act so macho in today's world. The bird and I gave each other the look.

We enjoyed the bird's company for a few hours, finally determining that he was dry and unsticky enough to be released back into the wild. We ignored those disturbing visions of an oriole stuck in the treetops. Outside we paraded. We stood in the middle of our yard, the oriole in no hurry to leave my finger.

My wife took the opportunity to give him another talk on the perils of gluttony. That did the trick. The bird gave me the look and flew to a nearby tree. He perched on a branch from whence he whistled and preened until the day darkened into night.

My wife and I searched each day for our pal. We thought we saw him high in the trees, nowhere near the jelly feeder.

In the Backyard

The rosy fingers of the sun cause the world to blink awake.

I hear the voice of an invisible singer and the world begins anew.

A robin calls, merrily, verily, see?

Birds endeavor to out-warble one another—sounding as if everything with feathers was attempting to find a place in the choir.

Birdcalls are enchanting and serene, yet provide enough mysteries to last a lifetime.

I hear the *cheer-cheer-cheer-pretty-pretty-pretty* call of the cardinal. It gives me goosebumps on a hot day.

I listen to the indigo bunting sing, *What, what? Where, where? Here, here. See it, see it?*

Hearing the song of a bird is like hitting a baseball on

the sweet spot of a bat.

The indigo bunting is a beautiful blue bird that offers mystique from afar and beauty up close.

It calls once more.

Hearts sing. Souls dance.

The Local Discovery Channel

I was in the Waseca Public Library.

Libraries are wonderful places, filled with information and wonder. I looked out a large window onto a park. It was a day of abundant white. The snow was deep.

I watched a gray squirrel struggle to move through the snow. A young red-tailed hawk was watching the squirrel with even more interest than I was.

The hawk flew down and grabbed the squirrel. It attempted to fly off with the squirrel, but had clutched it with only one talon. At about two feet off the ground, the squirrel dropped. The hawk made another attempt as the squirrel bounded through the snow. The hawk missed. The squirrel clambered up a tree and found a safe place. The hungry hawk flew away, still free for lunch.

The Downy Downs It

A downy woodpecker grabbed a sunflower seed from the feeder and flew to the deck of our house. It had discovered a chink in the wood's armor. The woodpecker inserted the sunflower seed into a small hole in the railing. Once the seed was properly in place, the woodpecker hammered it open.

By the end of the day, there was a small pile of hulls on the deck. It served as evidence of appetite.

They are Going Steady

The male cardinal, resplendent in his red finery, grabbed

a sunflower seed and offered it to a beautiful female cardinal. She accepted the gift demurely. Their bills touched. This is called mate-kissing. The sunflower seed had become an engagement seed.

From Over Here

A morning chorus greeted me as I walked some letters to the mailbox. Birdsong is nature's wake-up call. I never fully realize how much I miss that aubade until it returns each spring.

A red-tailed hawk flew by. A number of indignant red-winged blackbirds pursued it. The raptor was like a man with money hanging from his pockets being chased by luxury car salesmen.

Later in the day, I watched a family of crows hectoring a young bald eagle flying over a dead deer it hoped to feed upon.

Near the end of March, I saw 60 bald eagles on Geneva Lake, not far from my home. The eagles formed a circle on the ice surrounding open water. There they waited for fish to pop up. I knew how they felt.

Growing up, the kitchen was a destination for family members with appetites. We would migrate to the kitchen. Conversation was our declared intent, but we hovered near the oven waiting for something edible to pop up.

Nature by the Yard

A number of pheasants visit my feeders on a daily basis once the ground is covered with snow. One of this winter's roosters is missing his tail; his long ending sacrificed to an icy perch or to a predator. I nicknamed him Stubby. One of my Christmas wishes was that Stubby would have a warm rear end.

My wife and I joined the cats, Ethel and Purl, in staring out the window. Our voyeurism was at the amateur level when compared to the cats.

The subject of our attention in our cozy home on the day before Christmas was a chipmunk that had mounted an assault on the bird feeders during a lull between storms. Chipmunks are restless sleepers. They do not enter a deep hibernation and rely on the caches of food that they have brought to their burrows.

The chipmunk starring in our window's production emerged from its den to a multistoried (to it) cover of snow. If that wasn't challenge enough, it was chased by a fox squirrel—a creature of gargantuan proportions when compared to the chipmunk. It was frightened by a number of birds, especially by a young red-headed woodpecker with a gray-brown head. A flock of pheasants gave it cause to run and dive into a hole in the snow. A pair of starlings, battling in midair, accidentally fell upon it.

The chipmunk navigated an obstacle course of baffles and icy shepherd's hooks to obtain some sunflower seeds to fill its cheek pouches. The chipmunk hit the snow numerous times—falling from feeders and shepherd's hooks.

Frightened once again by the juvenile red-headed woodpecker, the chipmunk jumped from a feeder to a neighboring shepherd's hook in the hopes of scrambling to safety. Its rear foot became caught in the fork of the shepherd's hook. It struggled to free itself. Panic set in both outdoors and indoors. I was about to come to the chipmunk's rescue when it freed itself.

It was a good Christmas present.

Looking Out the Window

The cardinal is the early bird, but it doesn't come for worms. It visits the feeders early and then late, usually being the last bird of the day. It feeds on sunflower seeds when the day is quite dark. There is another bird that is a regular at my feeders, but sleeps late in the morning. It's the house sparrow.

The house sparrows had been absent from my yard during the spring, summer, and fall, but the harshness of winter brought them back. They chirp loudly, even on the coldest of days—those in which my digital thermometer is unable to go to where it needs to be to register the true temperature. House sparrows were called English sparrows when I was a boy, in reference to the homeland of the birds. It is difficult to find a fast food restaurant parking lot that is not inhabited by house sparrows. A friend calls them McDonald's sparrows.

Looking Out My Window

The juncos, cardinals, finches, woodpeckers, nuthatches, jays, and chickadees at my bird feeders were joined by three other visitors. The squirrel and the rooster pheasant were regulars, but the other was a stranger. It was an opossum. It appeared to have been faring well during the winter because its ears and tail were lacking the bright pink of frostbite.

The pheasant and the opossum shared the bounty that the squirrel threw down from a platform feeder until the opossum reared up and sniffed the air. It was plain to see that it coveted the seeds in a hanging feeder. It attempted to climb an icy shepherd's hook holding the feeder. The ice caused the opossum to slide down after a short climb. It fell to the snow, landing on its back, and became like an upside down turtle. It rocked its way to an upright position just as your favorite uncle does before getting up from his beloved easy chair.

The opossum made numerous attempts to scale the

hook with the same results each time. It ignored the seeds on the ground that were easy taking in order to go for the unattainable—which were the same kind of seeds.

Its actions reminded me of the wise words of another opossum, Pogo, who said, "We have met the enemy and he is us."

Flying Flowers

I looked at the sunflowers. There were many beautiful flower heads. As I watched, one of the flowers flew away. It was an American goldfinch—a tiny bird that is a symphony of song and feathers. To see a flower fly is a gift given only to the very young, the extremely fortunate, and the eccentric.

An Early Warning System

At the airports, travelers are told repeatedly that the threat level is orange. I listened to the blue jays cry in alarm in my yard. I'm not sure what upset them. To the blue jays, it is always a red alert.

A Hummingbird Haircut

I was at a tonsorial emporium. As I was being sheared, a hummingbird flew to the window of the barbershop and checked out the barber pole. The red of that pole attracted the tiny bird.

One Turkey Watches Other Turkeys

I was having a bowl of raisin bran. I was in that breakfast cereal trance. You know it. We eat spoonful after spoonful without spill but our minds are elsewhere. Suddenly, my meditation was interrupted by the sight of three wild turkeys frolicking on the lawn. As I gazed out the window, the turkeys jumped, flapped their wings, and cavorted. That's right, as I looked out my kitchen window, there were turkeys cavorting on my lawn. The neighborhood is changing.

Watching Birds from a Window

I write for a living. That means I need to spend time staring out the window.

The day was so cold that the rabbits were wearing earmuffs and snow fell in small flakes. I mumbled, "Little snow, big snow. Big snow, little snow," to myself. That meant that little flakes generally lead to more accumulation than do big flakes—winter wisdom wrought from years of Minnesota blizzards.

I watched as the house sparrows hit the bird feeders. A house sparrow is like that fussy kid in the highchair—the one more interested in making a mess than eating. House sparrows fight over the seed they don't eat. They toss the seeds they are unable to consume to the ground. They throw their food here and there. They'd be right at home at one of my family reunions.

Suddenly, the blue jays had a collective cow. They kicked up a fuss of epic proportions. Then they vanished, as did all the other birds at the feeders. The busy feeders became deserted as the birds took flight *en masse* into deep cover.

Winter is like swimming with sharks. It can be pleasant but there are always dangers. The disappearing act of the birds was a sign that an accipiter (Cooper's hawk or sharpshinned hawk) was near. As fast as they are, accipiters are built for maneuverability more than for speed. Chasing small birds through tight quarters can be hazardous. Many accipiters treated for injuries had suffered broken bones from such pursuits. I've read that raptors that eat mammals succeed in capturing prey only about 20 percent of the time. The success rate drops drastically for hawks attempting to catch birds. Birds are practiced escape artists and are difficult to seize. Studies have shown that bird-eating raptors succeed in catching prey only 7.6 percent of the time.

The yard was quiet with no perceptible movement of any kind. It was like the night before Christmas. Not a creature was stirring. I saw a nuthatch pressed motionless against the bark of a tree, involved in a serious game of freeze tag.

Then I saw a chickadee in a lilac. Its bill moved up, down, and around, as though the tiny bird was attempting to look in all directions at once. It pointed its bill as I do my nose in order to use my bifocals. While it was doing that, the chickadee sang its name, *Chick-a-dee-dee-dee-dee-dee-dee-dee-dee-dee*. The number of *dees* indicated the threat perceived by that minute bundle of feathers. I didn't see the hawk, but the chickadee told me that it was there.

I watched for 10 minutes as the chickadee kept an eagle eye out while constantly sounding an alarm. The *dees* were countless. Then the chickadee flew to the feeder and grabbed a sunflower seed. My mother had a short memory for bad things. She claimed it was the only way to be. Maybe that chickadee had the same kind of memory.

After the chickadee had made a few successful trips to the feeder, other birds returned. Juncos, goldfinches, tree sparrows, various species of woodpeckers, blue jays, house sparrows, and an unfrozen nuthatch.

The Cool Cat

The cats (Ethel and Purl) and I were staring out the window at a stray yellow tomcat with an oversized head. The cats that were sharing the view with me never set a paw outside. I wished the tomcat had a home to go to on a day featuring some of winter's worst traits.

A Bob Dylan song on the radio warbled, "Don't think twice, it's all right," as the cats and I watched the intruder plop down in the snow near the bird feeders.

Four hen pheasants moved in to feed on the corn that I had placed on the ground for them. The tomcat was near the corn and attempted to hold his ground. His eyes shifted nervously as the pheasants came closer. He was outnumbered. The tomcat did a stiff-legged walk away in a retreat. I'm sure that he was frightened but he didn't want to show it.

The pheasants gobbled the kernels of corn with gusto until the snowplow went by in yet another attempt to remove one more layer of snow from the road. The blade scraped loudly, snow flew in curtains, and the truck's engine growled.

The pheasants flew.

Ethel and Purl moved from the window and went off to take catnaps, convinced that the snowplow was the king of the jungle.

From Over Here

I galumphed my way to the bird feeders. I had to shovel some white stuff because the snow had become so deep that birds couldn't fly over it. The house sparrows had not been prominent in my yard for most of the year, but they moved in after Christmas like jobless relatives. My snow removal duties completed, I trudged back to the house, feeling valuable after making the world safe for bird feeding.

Safely ensconced in my home, I watched from my window as a gray squirrel ran at a crow that was feeding on the ground not far from the bushytail. The crow flew just far enough to escape the wrath of the angry squirrel. The squirrel was feeling good about itself, walking in a John Wayne swagger, when another crow flew from a nearby tree and buzzed the squirrel, scaring the sunflower seeds out of it.

Ben Gay

The early squirrel gets the sunflower seed.

They come early, the horde of squirrels. They need an early start because they have a lot of squirrel stuff to do.

I hear them on the roof of our house as I pretend to work in my office. It's the pitter-patter of little feet that attracts the attention of my faithful canine companion, Towhee. To her, it could just as well be elephants or Nazis on the roof as squirrels. Towhee has put herself in charge of the squirrel watch. She is the family's early warning squirrel system. She voices her concern with a series of woofs.

The squirrels tap dance on my roof. They take years off the life of my shingles.

Towhee is a bit of a bully and enjoys chasing tree squirrels. She doesn't do them much harm, because they are tree squirrels. She also likes to tree cats. Sometimes one of the cats stayed in the tree long after Towhee had lost interest. Driven by guilt brought on by my dog's actions and the pleas of my wife, I used to get a ladder and rescue the cats. The felines were always much less than grateful for my good deeds. I stopped this practice when it dawned on me that I had never once seen a cat skeleton in a tree.

I try to ignore the squirrels. I realize that walking on the roof of my house is a routine activity as far as one of these bushy-tailed beasts is concerned.

Towhee refuses to overlook their squirrelly actions. Her barking intensifies. The squirrels realize they are safe as long as my dog is inside and they are outside. They get busy. Squirrels have a lot of energy. They do not need caffeine.

Squirrels have to get on feeders. They believe that it is no sin to fail. It's only a sin not to make an attempt.

The squirrels get so close to the windows in my office that I can smell their acorn breath.

One day, the squirrels stormed my castle. I would estimate that there were squirrels from at least seven different zip codes in my yard. The word had gotten out. There was good food in the Batts' bird feeders.

Now, I like squirrels—they are athletic, acrobatic, energetic, and endearing entertainers. It would be a sad world without squirrels. I reward them for their company by providing them with corn.

We all have our bad habits. Squirrels have the bad habit of chewing up my bird feeders.

On this day, I was once again pretending to work in my office. I was watching one of our bird feeders. The bird activity there enthralled me in a way that small, bright, shiny objects do. It was while I was watching the feeder that the attack began.

It wasn't just any bird feeder. It was a state-of-the-art bird feeder. One that I picked up on sale for only $2,995.99 with a loan that was interest-free for the first three months. It was supposed to be a squirrel-proof feeder, but no one had told the squirrels. They worked in teams to assault my bird feeder.

This isn't what a guy wants to see while he's pretending to work. I became concerned.

My snazzy feeder hung from a shepherd's hook made by a wonderful neighbor who could make anything. A bird feeder in paradise. The squirrels scrambled up the shepherd's hook like it was an interstate highway especially made for squirrels. They added insult to injury by chewing up my fancy feeder. They did the damage and had no liability insurance to cover it.

I needed a bouncer at my bird feeder.

I decided on a plan of action without giving it much thought. It was a rash move. I found a tube of Ben Gay in our bathroom. Ben Gay is some smelly stuff that when rubbed on aching muscles is supposed to ease the discomfort. My wife had given it to me in an attempt to stifle my incessant whining about a softball-playing, weary, sore arm.

I went outside and as the bushytails scattered, I smeared some Ben Gay on the pole. The process made my eyes water and my nose run. I might have cackled fiendishly.

Back in my office, I watched intently out my window as a squirrel approached the coveted feeder. He might have been the state's best squirrel, if there is such a contest, but all I saw was a marauder.

The squirrel began to climb the pole holding the feeder. Once he got to the Ben Gay, he stopped his ascent. He slid down the hook, sniffing the sticky substance adhered to the pole, and paused at the base just long enough to lick one of his paws.

That was a poor decision.

Whoomp! All of the hair on his tail stood on end. The squirrel got the look I get when I try to do fractions. He ran off as though he were late for free peanut daiquiri night at the local adult beverage dispensary.

The squirrel continued to linger in my yard, but it never tried climbing that shepherd's hook again.

Now, what I did was not a good thing. I don't recommend that anyone do this. I am not proud of my actions, and I do feel sorry about what I did.

But sometimes a man has to do what he has to do— even if it involves Ben Gay.

The Good-Mood Bunting

The indigo bunting is my wife's favorite bird—it brings her great pleasure when it arrives each spring.

When the beautiful blue bird appears, it puts my wife in such a great mood, that I find it possible for me to do much less than I should be doing.

The indigo bunting is well on its way to becoming my favorite because of that.

When Sparrows Attack

I watched a tiny chipping sparrow fly to the ground. The chipping sparrow has a rusty cap, a flawless appearance that makes it look like it was carved from wood, and a song like a miniature sewing machine.

The sparrow grabbed a large green caterpillar in its bill. My thoughts wandered to green eggs and ham. The bird began to beat the unfortunate worm upon the ground. It slapped the worm against the soil. The bird apparently was on a diet where it fights with its food before eating it.

The worm looked too big for the bird, but it eventually succumbed to the avian martial arts (Come at me with a cankerworm!) and was swallowed by the sparrow.

Spring

Mark Beltaire wrote, "The nicest thing about the promise of Spring is that sooner or later, she'll have to keep it."

The spring migrants had arrived. Birds were chirping and burping. The birds provide a touch of wildness for everyone. A male cardinal sang, *what cheer, what cheer, cheer cheer cheer!* He sang in hopes of attracting a female cardinal. I wanted to get a closer look at the redbird, but I wasn't carrying my binoculars. A birder not carrying binoculars is a cardinal sin!

Rusty Blackbirds

I am willing to go where spring takes me. Spring magnifies the world. The swelling buds make trees look closer. My yard was knee-deep in birds. The earth renews in birdsong. Soon the robins will be singing before dawn. The only fertilizer my lawn receives is compliments of rabbits, but dandelions will bloom on my drug-free lawn. I watched an opossum take an undisciplined walk across my field of view. In a herd of cowbirds under my feeders, I spotted a couple of rusty blackbirds. The rusty is a rapidly declining species with a song like a rusty hinge. The appearance of the rusty blackbirds made my day. I know that life isn't a Norman Rockwell painting, but most days come close.

Window Feeders

I have come to depend upon not being able to depend upon the weather. I placed black-oil sunflower seeds wherever I'd seen a bird's bill in my yard. My seed bill would be enormous compared to the size of each bird's bill. Starlings, grackles, cowbirds, red-winged blackbirds, and rusty blackbirds fed on the ground like there would be no tomorrow. The peanut feeder filled blue jays, nuthatches, and chickadees. I like the small platform feeders attached to the windows via suction cups. I think they offer seed in an enticing way while discouraging birds from colliding with the window. People found an extra benefit this winter. When the snow was deep and the feeder was near a crank-out window, the feeder could be filled from indoors. This saved shoveling snow or trudging through the deep white stuff.

Squirrel Olympics

Some years back, my lovely wife bought me a new bird feeder.

She is always buying me bird feeders. She knows that bird feeders make me happy and putting them up keeps me out of her hair. She bought me a wonderful feeder. It was one of those with the suction cups that allow the feeder to be attached to a window. The feeder came equipped with two small trays to hold the seeds. Armed with a stepladder, a tape measure, and a level, I set out to mount the bird feeder on a window of my office.

I thought the office would be the perfect spot because I'm always more than willing to watch birds instead of working. I measured the window so I could place the feeder in the exact center of the window. I used the level to make sure the feeder was, well, level. I filled the feeder trays with black-oil sunflower seeds. I put the same number of seeds in each tray. It was scientific research. I planned to discover whether more birds were right-handed or left-handed. I put the stepladder, the tape measure, and the level away and went into my office.

I stood in the middle of my office, scratching my chin and admiring my handiwork. It was perfection. No one had ever done a better job putting up a bird feeder. Then I noticed him—a squirrel on the ground near my office. I knew the squirrel. He was always getting into my feeders, flinging seed every which way, and then chewing up my poor feeders. I recognized him by his one short ear. He was missing part of the ear—I figured he lost it in a fight or that it froze off during one of our nasty winters. He was a wily veteran. I watched the squirrel looking up at my new feeder perfectly placed in the center of my office window.

I could swear that I saw the squirrel scratching his chin.

I knew what was happening. The aggravating squirrel was doing geometric equations in his head. He was trying to figure out how to get from where he was to where my new feeder was located. I remember thinking that I had him this time. I thought that there was no way that the bushy-tail could get his paws on this feeder. I had a squirrel-proof feeder. There was an eave overhanging the window by some distance and an eavestrough (rain gutter) attached to the end of that. I knew the squirrel would try. That's its job.

I expected to hear the pitter-patter of little squirrel feet on the roof of my office, and I was not disappointed. I recognized his walk. I wasn't worried. I knew that, for once, I had this squirrel licked. There was no way he was going to get to my new feeder—the perfect feeder. I had to laugh a little as I watched the squirrel's furry head hanging down from the eavestrough as it peeked at the feeder. I watched as the squirrel hung by his rear toenails from the eavestrough. I kept watching as he began to swing back and forth. After much of this swinging, the squirrel made his move. He launched himself from the gutter towards the world's perfect feeder. He fell several feet short of his goal and plummeted to the ground. I almost felt sorry for him. If it had been any other squirrel, I would have had a little sympathy for him.

The blue jays were laughing at him and the chipmunks were chuckling at him. Squirrels are nothing if they are not optimistic. The squirrel gathered his bruised ego and pitter-pattered back onto my roof. Once again, I saw the little head eyeing my feeder. His eyes shifted back and forth rapidly. He was recalculating. I saw the swinging and the second launch of the squirrel. It was every bit as much of a failure as his first attempt. It was pitiful. A crowd had begun to gather—grackles, chickadees, woodpeckers, sparrows,

A LIFE GONE TO THE BIRDS

and rabbits. There is nothing quite as intriguing as a fallen hero. After each failure, the squirrel dusted himself off and climbed to the roof once more. I watched the squirrel fail and fall to the ground many times. I should have been working, but I was really enjoying the trials and tribulations that the furry pest was going through. I decided that I was going to watch one more attempt by the squirrel and then I was going to get on with my day.

I watched the squirrel's head drop from the trough. There was something different about it this time. The squirrel had a look in its eyes like the look an Olympic pole-vaulter has in his final attempt. The athlete knows that if he doesn't do it this time, he goes home without a medal. The squirrel had the same look.

I watched as the squirrel hung by its rear toenails and began to sway. Please don't attempt this at home. Squirrels are trained professionals. This time, when it launched its assault at my perfect feeder, the squirrel bent his little squirrel knees (if squirrels have knees) and pushed off from the eavestrough. The squirrel flew through the air with the greatest of ease until he smashed into my window like George of the Jungle hitting a tree. He hit face first. His upper lip caught on the glass. The rest of the squirrel joined the lip and slid down my office window leaving a trail of squirrel spit as it did so. He found his way to my squirrel-proof feeder.

The squirrel ignored my pounding on the window—he was a cagey veteran and knew that he was safe behind the invisible, protective shield—and ate his fill of the sunflower seeds. He threw seeds down to the jays who had been laughing at him and the chipmunks who had been chuckling at him. They bowed to him in a manner that demonstrated that they were not worthy.

Then to show his utter disdain for me, the squirrel took a big bite out of my new and perfect feeder.

The squirrel could get to the feeder any time he wanted to. All it took for him was a trip onto the roof, a couple of swings while hanging from the rain gutter, and a face-first crash into the window.

If squirrels were allowed into the Olympic Games, they would win all of the gold medals.

We can learn from squirrels. If we want something, we should not give up easily.

Playing those Swallow Games

It was early in the day when I saw them: a pair of tree swallows and a large, white feather. The swallows were flying high overhead. One carried the feather in its bill. It released the feather and the other swallow zoomed in and grabbed the feather in midair. I watched as the pair repeated this activity in the sky. Playing with nest materials is likely a part of the pair bonding process. It was a beautiful thing to see and it made me smile. Later in the day, I walked under a utility wire running above a nest box favored by tree swallows. I looked up to see a swallow perched on the wire. It appeared unconcerned with my proximity. I walked to the mailbox, and on my stroll back to the house I noticed that the swallow, still perched in the same location, became excited and vocal. I looked up to see its partner flying into the yard. It had a large, white feather in its bill.

In the Backyard

I walked a gauntlet of spider webs as I listened to the robins *tut-tutting* from a mulberry tree. Tree swallows, nesting in my yard, clicked their bills at me as they flew by. I could almost hear Cat Stevens singing, "I'm being followed by a tree swallow." The red on the head of a red-headed woodpecker caught the sun. As I watched the handsome woodpecker feed on sunflower seeds, the rest of the world seemed out of focus.

A Kiss from a Thrasher

It was that last bit of twilight before the world outside became dark enough to hide most of its secrets.

I heard a sound like that of a loud, smacking kiss.

I recognized the call as that of the brown thrasher. A brown thrasher has one of the largest repertoires of songs of all our common birds. Its song is an attractive series of loud musical phrases, each phrase usually repeated, the whole song often continuing for several minutes at a time. Some listeners use the mnemonic "Drop-it, drop-it; cover-it-up, cover-it-up; pull-it-up, pull-it-up." They repeat themselves just as I do.

The brown thrasher is slim-bodied and long-tailed. It is rufous above, with a soft white throat, breast, and belly with brown streaking, and buffy flanks. The bill is fairly long and the adults have bright yellow eyes. It is a striking beauty, the state bird of Georgia, and has a hockey team in Atlanta named after it.

An aggressive defender of its nest, the lanky brown thrasher has been known to strike cats, dogs, raccoons, and, occasionally, people.

I listened to that constant lip smacking. I hadn't heard so much since the last lutefisk feed I attended.

My wife and I searched for the reason for the vocalizations—the purpose of the alarm calls. We saw it. It was a mother raccoon and baby. The raccoon is an eater of baby birds and eggs.

It's difficult to be too critical as I eat eggs myself, but we joined the thrasher team and chased the raccoons away.

The comments from the thrashers ceased.

Not long after that night, I walked near a nest box housing tree swallows. I wanted to check on the babies, and I enjoy looking at cute things. As I peered at the brood, a swallow parent, an elegant flyer, dive-bombed me. Its attack strategy was a swoop, hang a left turn, swoop—repeat as necessary. It flew close enough that I could hear the click of its bill and feel the whoosh of its wings on my hair.

I felt like I needed a hard hat.

I'm glad raccoons don't wear them.

Chapter 4:
When Nature Calls

It Pays to Listen

A man from Illinois told me that when he and his friend go looking at warblers each spring, they listen to tapes of songs of the warblers as they travel in a car. After listening to eight hours of such tapes, they arrived at a woods filled with warblers. The first call of a warbler they heard stumped them for an instant before the friend said, "Disc two, cut three."

The End of a Coot

I was looking at waterfowl floating on a lake. A bald eagle flew over the water. The eagle's appearance caused a bit of panic among the birds on the water. I watched as the eagle flew near a raft of coots. Coots are often called mudhens and bald eagles love to eat coots. The eagle zeroed in on one particular coot. As the raptor closed in on its prey, I yelled involuntarily, "Duck!"

The eagle captured the coot.

I should have yelled, "Coot!"

Counting Hawks

Sometimes, as I travel alone on long road trips, I count hawks on posts and utility wires. There is no purpose to this game. It is an idle diversion that doesn't detract from the attention paid to driving.

Wear Your Binoculars as a Badge of Honor

The duct tape on my bag shows the evidence of prolonged use.

I feel like a tattered airline tag, but those in my company inspire me.

I look back at the wonderful group of folks following me down the birding trail. They look like an army of birders—uniformed and at the ready.

I call birds flying over. They remind me of Pete Dunne's advice. Pete says that you can call a bird anything you want as long as it's flying away, but if it turns around and heads back towards you, you'd better be right.

After we complete our trip checklists, I remind all that they should wear their binoculars to lunch. I want them to let people know that they are getting business from birders. So all birders should wear binoculars in public as much as possible, unless they are lousy tippers. Lousy tippers should leave their binoculars in their cars.

A Traveling Man

I was having lunch with a friend in the Lower Rio Grande Valley of Texas. We were discussing the amazing diversity of birdlife in that part of the world.

My friend became excited about the birds we'd seen and the birds we'd see. He blurted out, "I didn't believe it until now, but everything in Texas really is bigger!"

The words had no sooner left his mouth than we both looked up into the eyes of an annoyed 300-pound waitress.

The Rented Bird

We were looking at shorebirds and I pointed out a particular species.

"Leased sandpiper?" said one in the group. "That's a rented bird?"

It was a least sandpiper.

A Warbler Walk

As I walked a bridge across the Root River at Forestville State Park on May 1, my steps were to the song provided by a yellow warbler. My father called it the "summer warbler." Memories of my father and his appreciation of birds made me smile. The tiny bird provided a delightful song, breathtaking beauty, and pleasant memories. It put a spring in my step. This yellow jewel amid the tree leaves was the only warbler I encountered that day at Forestville, but it was a good one.

Hot Licks

The sky was as blue as any baby's eyes.

The heat was of such intensity that it felt as though my inner child was playing with matches.

I don't believe in living life with my brakes on even on a hot July day.

I was volunteering at a couple of state parks on this day. I love our state parks, but leading people around in the stifling heat might be less than the fun it should be. I considered my endeavor a penance I needed to pay for hitting a butterfly with my pickup.

As I exited my truck upon my arrival at a park, I could almost hear the Buckinghams singing "Kind of a Drag."

Shortly thereafter I was met by a large group of folks— each one apparently as nuts as I was.

We began to walk in search of avian treasures.

The birdsong became noticeable in its absence. Even the neighborhood alarmist, the blue jay, became shut-mouthed in the excessive heat.

I was about to do some yodeling, when instead I rejoiced in the nearly constant song of the indigo bunting. The tiny, feathered beauty voiced, *Fire, fire. Where, where? Here, here. See it, see it?*

His performance was a crowd-pleaser.

It's difficult to walk away from a singing bird—even on a day so hot that shadows melt.

The song of a bird must be heard. If not, it is like a book without a reader, a diminished thing.

The quiet was further kept at bay by the trumpeting *garoo* of sandhill cranes.

I applauded their vocal efforts. They and the fine folks walking with me made a miserable day sparkle.

Valdez Values

A friend and I were sitting on an open porch in Valdez, Alaska. It had been a long day of travel filled with incredible sights.

We were too amazed to eat or sleep.

We sat with our feet up, binoculars around our necks, and hope in our eyes.

We watched the next day's weather sneak past the mountains surrounding the city.

We employed the binoculars to look at birds when we needed to, but mostly we talked and listened. I enjoyed the company of another who liked looking the same direction I did.

"We are lucky to be able to enjoy the simple pleasures," I said.

"True, true," my friend responded. "It's like we've been cursed, only in a good way."

I couldn't have agreed more.

What?

I listened to the Canada geese at a State Park the other day. The geese sounded like callers to a talk radio station. They were outraged. When they calmed down, I could still hear the whispered mutterings between the birds. I think geese have trouble hearing subdued voices, because they kept repeating, *Huh*?

Why Not Let It Order Off the Menu?

While I was speaking at the Kirtland's Warbler Festival in Roscommon, Michigan, a man told me about his trip to Florida.

When he checked into the place he was staying in, the proprietor told him not to feed the heron steak.

The man thought that was odd introductory advice and asked for an explanation.

It seems there was a great blue heron that hung around the docks near the hotel.

Some of the guests had begun to feed the heron hot dogs.

The bird liked them.

The owner of the hotel began to provide hot dogs for the guests to feed to the bird.

It was a slight tourist attraction. Not many hotels could offer a hot dog-eating heron.

Then one day, a guest gave the heron a kosher hot dog.

The heron liked the kosher hot dogs much better than the hot dogs he'd been getting before—so much so that it would no longer eat regular hot dogs.

The innkeeper was forced to start providing kosher hot dogs for the guests to feed the bird. The kosher hot dogs were, of course, pricier than the other hot dogs.

That is why the hotel owner asked every guest to not feed the heron steak.

The Returning

We are not promised an easy life. Neither are bald eagles. For an eagle, the living is never too easy. Things happen.

I was in Haines, Alaska, to watch a release of bald eagles that had been rehabilitated and deemed ready to be returned to the wild.

Bald eagles gather along the Chilkat River outside Haines to feed on chum salmon in open waters during the fall and winter.

The bald eagle is our national bird. Perhaps because of that, it is as much a legend as a bird. The bird is the embodiment of freedom. The personification of the American dream.

It was a cold, short day. Light was in short supply. As I drove to the release site, the local public radio station played country music featuring songs about misbehaving people in need of forgiveness.

The eagles I was about to see released were birds that had made mistakes. They were birds that were victims of misfortune. Accidents had robbed them of their ability to fly for a time, but thanks to the work of caring and committed rehabilitation experts, the eagles would be returned to the wild.

A friend from California, Preston Cook, was one of those fortunate souls whose generosity allowed him to release a bald eagle several years ago. Releasing the eagle was a life-changing event for Preston. He told me that the experience is a part of each and every one of his days.

Many folks gathered at the point of release. Most all were sporting cameras. For the wildlife artist or photographer, the bald eagle is his or her inevitable subject.

It was a frigid day of blue, white, and gray. Noses ran in the cold. Feet attempted to stay warm by stamping in the snow. Eyes teared, not from the temperature, but from the occasion, as the lives of the eagles to be released were reviewed in detail.

The eagles were transported in pet carriers. I watched intently as the first of which had its door opened at a location facing the Chilkat River.

There was a moment's hesitation as the eagle questioned its good fortune. A seductive pause to the viewers. Then it burst into the air with the suddenness of a flipped switch into a flight followed by hundreds of eyes.

Camera shutters clicked as human hearts ticked. The rapid blinking cameras capturing the moment. Taking photographs is a cheap method of buying the perfect day.

A feathered flight to freedom. An exquisite elegance.

For an instant, the eagle became a bronzed statue in flight. A flash of sun highlighted its escape. An eerie brilliance of dreamscape. Innocent and intimidating at the same time. The eagle went back to where it belonged. Freed to live a life of salmon dinners.

Other eagles were released.

The birds flew with a resolve as though the prospect of paradise awaited them. Each eagle flew with a sense of purpose. They flew as if they understood. They got it. The eagles underwent an accelerated transition from restrained to excitement.

We watched the eagles away.

Like a puff of smoke, the eagles were gone from our sight, but they will linger forever in our hearts.

The release created feelings more powerful than words could convey.

I felt mad with delight as I saw eagles reflected in the eyes of the people near me.

No one said a farewell. The thoughts were a collective, "Welcome home!"

I could almost hear some country crooner croaking out a song about misbehaving eagles who needed forgiveness.

Life is a knotted tapestry, laced with severity. We hope for redemption.

We sometimes travel without ever arriving, but there are those special moments.

An opportunity to see the release of a bald eagle into the wild is a temptation that should not be resisted. You can't remember tomorrow.

The release changed lives—both avian and human.

It was one of those marvelous occasions when hopes and dreams coincided with reality.

It gave us all reason to wake up hopeful.

North Dakota

We were near Chase Lake in North Dakota. It's the home of more pelicans than could be counted. I watched Forster's terns and common terns fly over. Forster's terns are much more common than the common terns. Snipe and shrikes appeared—Wilson's snipe and loggerhead shrikes (butcherbirds). I pointed at two shrikes on a utility wire. A fellow traveler added quickly, "Three shrikes and you're out."

The motor coach in which the participants in the Potholes and Prairies Festival were traveling became stuck on a gravel road made slick by a constant rain. I have experienced this before. I have stepped off immobile motor coaches from Fairbanks, Alaska to Roscommon, Michigan to Meadowlands, Minnesota to Carrington, North Dakota. Each time, I was amazed at the number of folks who cheerfully get off the bus and push.

I looked at three shrikes and we were out.

Christmas Bird Count 2009

I was on the road before the snowplows and after the snowfalls.

There was no scarcity of cold or snow. The weather held as cold as a January gravestone. It was icier than a Tiger Woods family portrait.

I knew the winter was going to be bad when all the leaves flew south.

I give myself a gift each year—a Christmas Bird Count (CBC). I do more than one. I'm big on giving.

People used to do a Christmas Side Hunt by shooting birds and then counting them. Frank Chapman had the idea in 1900 of counting the birds without shooting them. Genius!

I drove and walked while searching for birds or *brrrrrrds*. I love walking even when the wind blows the whiskers off my face. It builds my appetite for mashed potatoes. The mashed-potato rule applies to counting birds. I could never have all the mashed potatoes I want to eat and I could never see all the birds I want to see. My driving threatened no speed limit and I walked gingerly on treacherous paths like a cow going past a butcher shop.

Christmas Bird Counts give my mother-in-law the opportunity to tell my wife, "I told you so."

The wonderful Welsh poet William H. Davies wrote, "What is this life if, full of care, we have no time to stand and stare." He could have been doing a CBC. I look for birds the way Mrs. Kravitz—the nosey neighbor on "Bewitched"—looked for gossip.

I enjoy counting birds. It reduces the stress I would feel if I were not counting birds. It gives me the opportunity to display the math skills that garnered me a C- minus on an arithmetic test and earned me the reputation as the family brain. The counts I participate in produce numbers somewhere between those of Prudhoe Bay, which has one bird species on its CBC (the common raven), and those counts in South Texas that would be disappointed with fewer than 150 species.

A CBC is citizen science at its coolest. I'm trying to save the planet by counting birds. How do I do it? I count the legs and divide by two. A CBC is like a round of golf without clubs and with the higher score being the better. It's a time to find joy in seeing a common grackle. Every bird is a bird. Every feathered individual counts. Zero means everything and it means nothing on a CBC. Zero chickadees would be catastrophic. Zero kiskadees in Minnesota wouldn't be much of a surprise.

Research has shown that forcing yourself to smile can improve your mood. I don't have to force a smile while doing a CBC. It's like a pie-eating contest, only without the need to wear a plastic garbage bag.

Counting birds is a bold adventure. I've done a CBC while wearing a suit and tie so I could attend a funeral in the middle of the count. I've counted in the company of a Chihuahua wearing a sweater. I've counted birds from a Chevy Vega while trying to avoid drivers who thought they owned the potholes. I've been outside when it was icy and slippery enough that I had to bird on all fours. I've been stopped by police officers for being a suspicious character. I've had both a heater and a defroster stop working (it's a family tradition to be the last owner, not counting the junkyard, of every car). I've used out-of-focus binoculars that gave me a headache. I've peered through blizzards while trying to see a snowy owl. I've become stuck in a mountain of snow and was thankful that a shovel is standard birding equipment. Birds warm me.

Many birds flee from our winters. Birders add plumage—long underwear, wool socks, stocking caps, and mittens. The secret is to accessorize. I was the compiler of a count that featured an American white pelican for a number of years. That's no big deal for many counts, but for Minnesota, it's a nice bird. The pelican had a bad wing and couldn't fly. He was unable to convince another pelican to overwinter. He became lonely and fell in love with a domestic white goose. She wasn't good for him. We could all see it, but he thought she was all it. She dumped him for a gray gander without a job. We knew it would happen. The pelican was found floating dead in the lake one spring day. I can't help but blame her.

I believe that counting birds is good for the economy, and this is backed up by Federal Reserve Chairman and *Time Magazine*'s 2009 Person of the Year, Ben Bernanke, who, when asked for comment, replied with an insightful, "Huh?"

I am a CBC compiler of long standing. Each individual counter is important. You can't have a river without each drop of water. Until they perfect the self-counting bird, I'll be counting. If we don't count birds, who will? CBC? COM—Count On Me.

I know what counts—birds and those who count them.

Gulls

We have many gulls and they are important to Minnesota. Some of us have been fortunate enough to spend time around Gull Lake. There is a plethora of businesses and resorts that carry "gull" in their names. There is a city named East Gull Lake and, of course, a river named the Gull River. Some of us are gullible. A book titled *Jonathan Livingston Seagull* sold well. We tend to call the gulls, "seagulls." They are not really seagulls, and that may be what they are complaining about with all their squawking. They might be more appropriately called landfill gulls. We don't have a sea in my neck of the woods, but we do have gulls. If I see a gull along a river, it is a rivergull. Along a lake, it's a lakegull. If a gull is spending time in a bay, it's a baygull.

Birding a Pear Tree

I was walking around the riverfront area in La Crosse, Wisconsin. It was a beautiful fall day and the spot was busy with people. I stopped to admire a pear tree. A bird flew from the tree. It was not a partridge. It was a house sparrow. A sparrow in a pear tree.

Chickadeed

I spotted a chestnut-backed chickadee in Juneau, Alaska. It looked like a black-capped chickadee with a sooty-brown cap instead of a black one, and with a chestnut-colored back, shoulders, and sides. I pulled my camera from its case and took a photo of the lovely bird. A vital cord for the camera fell unnoticed from my bag. I get excited about seeing chickadees. There should be a name for my condition—something like "chickadeeitis." I wasn't aware of the missing cord until that night when I returned to my room and bath. Darkness had fallen with a thud when I grabbed my trusty flashlight (a welcome traveling partner) and hiked far back to the spot where I had enjoyed the company of the chickadee. I found the lost cord and returned to my room and bath with pleasant thoughts. I'd definitely been chickadeed.

Wow!

We watched hundreds of bald eagles gathered along the

Chilkat River near Haines, Alaska. A momentary abundance of birds that made precious dreams come true. I asked a fellow eagle watcher what she thought of her first visit to the Valley of the Eagles.

Her reply was, "Wow!"

That small word described perfectly what we were seeing in our biggest state.

Made You Look

I was dressed like a buffoon—dressing that way is the secret to cold weather survival—when it happened.

I was in Alaska and had that feeling that I was being watched. I suspected it was Sarah Palin and I was trying to spot her when a bald eagle flew overhead and landed in a nearby tree.

"Why do birds, suddenly appear, whenever you are near..." sang my lovely wife in a key yet to be embraced by the music industry.

Eagles fly over my head at my home in Minnesota. Most things go over my head. Those eagles don't often land near me. They land in places close to me but not when I'm there.

This one was a regal eagle, befitting its position as our national bird. I looked at the treed eagle. The eagle looked at me. It had the hint of a sneer. I recognize sneers—I have in-laws. I captured its image with my eyes and had it developed in my brain's darkroom. It's the largest room in my mind. I employed a real camera, too, because I worried that my brain would misplace the photo and there was little chance it'd be ready when promised.

I used my new digital camera. I had to buy a new camera after my cousin hit me over the head with my Polaroid instant camera, claiming that taking his picture would steal his soul. Odd behavior for a Lutheran. My new device has a zoom, so I can take bad photos from great distances. The photos of the raptor turned out swell. I blame that on the subject—a bald eagle perched in a leafless cottonwood with a mountain powdered in November snow as the background. It was similar to that single Christmas ornament in Charlie Brown's tree—only the tree wasn't stunted like Charlie's. I doubt that digital cameras will ever catch on, but I was happy I had one with me. I could have used the camera in my smarter-than-me phone, but I prefer using it for taking portraits of my hand.

I was in Haines, Alaska. If the movie, *Trains, Planes and Automobiles* had been titled *Boats, Planes and Automobiles* and the lead characters (played by John Candy and Steve Martin) were both played by me, that film would depict my journey to Haines in November. Haines is where more eagles than I could count are present each November. And I can count.

Some have described Haines as quirky. If it is, it's probably why I feel so at home there. It doesn't seem quirky to me. It seems delightful. The American Bald Eagle Foundation is located in Haines. They offer a festival, programs, live birds, live people, and a gift shop.

Haines is where eagles are numerous and cats are nervous. A tomcat I know spends a lot of time looking up. Cats eat birds, and attentive cats worry about being eaten by birds.

The Chilkat River is where the eagles feed on weary salmon flailing about in open water. When eagles attack is not a documentary. It's a buffet. An interesting aside, I could find no documented record of a salmon ever attacking an eagle. That makes me go "hmmm."

The area is a photographer's dream. Shutters shudder in glee. People come from around the world to view eagles.

The Haines area is so scenic that it makes you look—it fills holes in lives.

A teen, jaded by his lack of years, stood beside me as I looked at the eagle in the cottonwood tree. He smiled and said, "Awesome!"

I returned the smile and said the word of my generation, "Cool."

Everyone should go to Haines. We all have to go some time. You should go to Haines first. I've been going to Haines for years. Each year, I think that nothing could top my last visit.

Each year, I say, "That was even better than last year."

Road to Nowhere

Some years ago, the first bald eagle nest that anyone could remember was discovered on a lake near my home.

I had driven my pickup down a gravel road to get my daily look at the two eaglets. It was a road that some claimed lead to nowhere. The road meandered by farm fields and large dogs—the kind of dogs that wag on one end and growl on the other. The nest tree was quite a distance from the road and I found the perfect spot for a spotting scope.

I pulled my pickup over onto the side of the road. I climbed out of my Chevy, a cup of hot tea in my hand, and I glassed the large nest with my binoculars. The baby eagles looked tiny in the enormous nest. I saw no other vehicles in the area. I heard no cars. The only sounds were the cawing of crows, the discussions of red-winged blackbirds, and a John Deere tractor working at hauling away part of the horizon. It was a place where a spotting scope could thrive.

I got the scope out of the truck and set it up on the road. I focused it on the nest and, as I am every time I look through a scope, I was amazed at what I saw. It took my breath away. I was so taken with what I saw, that I didn't notice that I was not alone. A large canine of the Heinz 57 variety had been attracted by my strange human behavior. He made his presence known by giving me an early Christmas goose, if you know what I mean. It's the way dogs shake hands.

I'm not a nervous person, but this action startled me, causing me to bang my eye sharply against the eyepiece of the scope while at the same time dumping the steaming contents of my teacup onto the crotch of my pants. The sound "Aaaiiieee!" came screaming from somewhere, perhaps from the deep, dark recesses of me.

This anguished cry frightened my new close friend. The mutt decided to make a run for safety by passing through the legs of my tripod. His escape plan had one minor flaw—the dog was too large to be able to run through a tripod. The dog scurried away with his tail tucked firmly between his legs as my scope tipped and prepared to hit the gravel. I dove for my precious scope, catching it right before it hit the ground in a diving snag that would have made any NFL All-Pro receiver proud.

I watched the dog giving me the evil eye from what he measured to be a safe distance. I sighed. I had a scraped elbow, a throbbing knee, a gouged eye, and a wet crotch. The scope had none of those things.

I resumed looking at the nest and was so mesmerized that I didn't hear the Buick pull up behind me until the driver honked an incredibly loud horn.

Fortunately, I had just switched the eye I was using on the scope, making it possible for me to smash my good eye into the eyepiece. No pro wrestler has ever suffered such an eye gouge. My eyes were a matched set. I heard car doors open and slam shut while I bit my tongue to keep from letting another "Aaaiiieee!" escape from my lips.

"What are you doing?" boomed a loud voice.

"Wawing babu ergos," I mumbled in reply, the words stumbling out from a bleeding tongue. It was supposed to come out as, "Watching baby eagles."

"Wawing babu ergos?" asked the voice.

I forced one eye open using my good hand—the one not sharing an arm with a wounded elbow. I made out the blurry figure of a man. He was a mountain of a man—a mountain with three hills. I assumed the hills were a wife and children. The kids giggled about the wet area on the front of my trousers. I heard the mother's words "accident" and "the poor man can't help it" in explanation.

I pulled a notepad and pencil from my pocket. It was a chance to display the penmanship that earned me a C- in the 5th grade. I scratched out a note to the man providing me with shade that informed him that I was watching baby eagles not wawing babu ergos. I made it clear that I had never wawed babu ergos—at least, not since I'd been married.

The Buick family held a short meeting, decided that I was a harmless, but troubled, incontinent man with small eyes and a speech impediment.

I offered them the use of my scope. They each looked through it and each look brought a smile.

The scope had claimed four more victims who would never look at a bird in the same way.

The man told me of a newspaper coupon for adult diapers and wished me luck with my problems. The family got into their Buick and drove off. The dog eyed me suspiciously from his home turf.

I welcomed a chance to spend quality time with my spotting scope. A time for my zipper to rust, my tongue to scab over, and my eyes to blacken. I watched as a parent eagle brought lunch to the babies.

All my problems were forgotten. Until I heard the beeping horn of a sneaky Toyota.

The Wood Thrush

I was walking down a far from beaten path through the woods when I heard it. It was a haunting, ethereal, flute-like song.

Ee-o-lay.

Liquid, rich, and melodic.

Frito-Lay.

The bird is reddish-brown above, white with large black spots below. It's built like a robin, only smaller.

Henry David Thoreau wrote, "The thrush alone declares the immortal wealth and vigor that is in the forest. Whenever a man hears it, he is young, and Nature is in her spring. Wherever he hears it, it is a new world and a free country, and the gates of heaven are not shut against him."

My father called it the "Swamp Angel" and it arrives when the wildflowers emerge in earnest. When it does, it becomes ear candy.

Pileated Woodpecker

I was leading a field trip.

The objective was to see birds.

I had a bone to pick with the day.

The day had been one of wall-to-wall rain. The weather had been miserable. The day had been a series of downpours interrupted only briefly by hope. The tattoo of raindrops on the roofs of the cars had been our constant companion. If the day had a theme song, it would have been, "Here Comes That Rainy Day Feeling Again."

As the rain refused to go away, the leader lost his confident swagger. The group sensed this. There was no threat of mutiny, but there were no high-fives either.

We stopped for a restroom break. It was a restroom made for birders. Trees and water surrounded the building. I chose the location because I am a big believer in the old saying, "If you gotta go, go somewhere nice."

As folks waited their turns, I scanned the area for anything avian.

One of the best things about birds is that they are everywhere. If we make the habit of looking, we will see. It is amazing what we can see by looking.

I heard the call. It sounded almost like a flicker, but not quite. It was the same wild laugh, only louder.

I saw a large bird fly into a nearby tree. A pileated woodpecker! The pileated has a flight that is unusually deliberate for a woodpecker.

I quickly found the bird with my naked eyes and then added my binoculars to reinforce the sighting. My binoculars became Gandalf, magically placing the bird in my eyes. Seeing the male bird with its red moustache was like looking at an exquisite painting.

The crow-sized pileated woodpecker played that woodpecker peek-a-boo with my eight-powered eyesight. It peered around one side of the tree and then the other.

As a boy, I was told that there are two kinds of people in the world. There are those who walk into a room and say, "Here I am." Then there are those who walk into a room and say, "There you are." I was told to strive to be a member of the latter group.

Seeing the pileated, I could almost hear the bird saying, "There you are."

I have always loved woodpeckers. My mother told her children that they could become whatever they wanted to be.

I decided I was going to become a woodpecker. It seemed to be a noble calling.

I received all kinds of advice from the older children.

One told me that I needed to practice.

I whined in response that I was not going to jump off the roof of the house again. It had taken my broken leg forever to heal and my parents were still paying the doctor's bill.

My helpful advisor agreed that I'd never be much of a flyer, but was adamant that I still needed to practice. He told me that woodpeckers hammered on trees and that was what I should learn to do. A kind-hearted lad, he told me that I should start out on a nice, soft tree like the stately bur oak that stood in our farmyard.

I think that's why I admire woodpeckers so much. When I think of all the headaches and bloody noses they had to go through to become what they are, I feel humbled.

Shakespeare said, "What's in a name?" Pileated can be pronounced either "pie-lee-ated" or "pill-e-ated." "Pileated" means "crested."

Everyone in our group got good looks at the most accommodating woodpecker.

To see the exquisite beauty of a bird such as the pileated woodpecker is reason enough to own binoculars.

On a dismal day, the pileated woodpecker brought sunshine to a flock of birders.

The pileated woodpecker was a gift; as was the company of people who appreciated its presence.

All of nature is holy. The cathedrals are not only the preserved habitats, but also the birds themselves.

They aren't rare birds, but seeing any bird makes for a rare moment.

Birds need special places. If we make sure they have these special places, we, in turn, will have our own special places.

Even when we stop to use a restroom.

Not All Birds are Created Eagle

I was seated in a form-fitting airplane, attempting to complete a journey from Juneau to Haines. I expected to see hundreds of eagles in Haines. As the small airplane neared its destination, I looked out my window in the hopes of losing some of the tiredness that had engulfed me and I saw an eagle flying nearby. It was a surreal moment. The beautiful bird buoyed my spirits.

I live in Minnesota. Why would any man who has been described as "almost normal" want to go north in November? I was in Alaska to speak at the wonderful Bald Eagle Festival. I had dreamed of going to Haines and seeing the eagles since the second grade.

Alaska. It's roomy and the weather is not always good-natured. Its famous snowman is named Permafrosty.

Everything in Alaska is farther apart than you'd think. The state is seven times the size of Minnesota and 470 times the size of Rhode Island. Weather and geography are travel challenges.

There is a lot to find in Alaska, but there is a lot of Alaska to find it in. Alaska is so big that when I went to an echo point and yelled, "Hello," it took 8 hours and 32 minutes for it to reply. Alaska is where brooks babble and glaciers are the size of a dream.

Haines is a small, remote community located in the Chilkat Valley, north of Juneau at the same northerly latitude as Oslo, Norway. It is in the Inside Passage, America's longest fjord, in Southeastern Alaska. It is 30 to 40 minutes by a small commuter plane or three to five hours by ferry from Juneau. The ferry is a delightful method of travel. It's a way to add nautical miles to a life's travels. From Seattle it is a 1.5-hour flight to Ketchikan and then another .5-hour to Juneau. Ketchikan receives 151 inches of precipitation annually on average. Seattle, notoriously drizzly, receives only 39 inches. Haines averages about 133 inches of snow per year, with the coldest temperature on record being -17 degrees F and the record high being 90 degrees. The winter temperature is typically in the 20 – 30 degree range.

As one who believes that the secret to surviving cold weather is to dress like a dork, I feel right at home in Alaska. People in Haines dress for the weather, not for style. If a man attempted to dress for the weather in Haines, he would need nine suitcases. The weather conditions changed rapidly during my stay. Snow, rain, cold, wind, sun, clouds, and ice each took a turn.

Haines features whiskered faces and hat hair. Men with eight pounds of beard are able to walk upright. Haines has no malls, no fast food restaurants, no big-box stores, no rush hour, and no stoplights. Haines is small, but not squished. Mt. Ripinsky looms 3,600 feet above downtown. Haines has glaciers, mountains, bears, five kinds of salmon, and bald eagles.

One of my favorite writers, Aldo Leopold, wrote, "Our ability to perceive quality in nature begins, as in art, with the pretty. It expands through successive stages of the beautiful to values as yet uncaptured by language." Haines is pretty.

It is difficult to find words to describe the thousands of bald eagles that gather along a stretch of the Chilkat River near Haines from October to February (peak numbers generally occur in November). The eagles are attracted by a late run of spawning chum salmon. Warm water keeps about five miles of the river ice-free throughout the winter.

I watched an eagle, trying to eat a salmon it had caught, fight with another eagle over the catch of the day. While they were fighting, a gull snuck in and began to eat the fish. Then a raven chased the gull off and began to dine on salmon. The original catcher of the salmon, having vanquished its challenger, flew back and chased the raven away. While the eagle was attempting to eat the salmon, quick and courageous magpies darted in and out, grabbing bills full of salmon. It was like visiting a popular buffet.

The Chilkat Bald Eagle Preserve was formed in 1982 and contains 48,000 acres set aside for the protection of the eagles. A good number of eagles call this "Valley of the Eagles" their year-around home. There are so many eagles that every cat in Haines looks up nervously.

Bald eagles were once fair game for hunters. Worried that the eagles' love of fish might deplete the salmon population, the Alaska Territorial Legislature offered a bounty on eagles in 1917. The price paid for each pair of talons ran $1-2. The bounty was removed in 1953, but not until more than 128,000 eagles had been shot for the bounty. When Alaska became a state in 1959, the bald eagles came under federal protection.

Dave Olerud, the founder of the American Bald Eagle Foundation located in Haines, said, "The bald eagle is an indicator, a litmus test. If the bird is healthy, man is healthy."

The eagles that had filled my dreams had become a reality. Other birds made themselves seen—black-billed magpies, ravens, trumpeter swans, and Steller's jays. I relished the song of the American dipper, sounding like a melody of wren and thrush songs. That it can sing after walking along the bottom of fast-moving, cold streams impressed me.

John Muir, who came to Haines in 1879 and was one of the first non-natives to explore the region, advised young people not to visit the area. He warned that they'd have to stay or realize that every other place they'd see would be a disappointment.

The bald eagle is our national bird. Perhaps because of that, it is as much a legend as a bird. The bird is the embodiment of freedom, the personification of the American dream. It made my grade-school dream come true.

Someone told me that Haines was a humble place. I think they meant that it was small. It is a humbling place. Humility doesn't mean you think less of yourself. It means you think of yourself less. With so many regal eagles around, a man cannot help but think of something other than himself.

My humble opinion is that some of the best views in the world are framed by windows in Haines, Alaska.

For more information on the American Bald Eagle Foundation, visit **baldeagles.org**.

Snowy Owls

I tried to do a nice thing at an airport. I volunteered without request to relinquish my seat on a plane to a serviceman headed home. I expected no compensation. It seemed like the right thing to do. It was going as planned until the flight was canceled due to mechanical problems.

Norm Smith, director of Massachusetts Audubon's Blue Hills Trailside Museum, has been doing nice things at airports for years. Smith monitored snowy owls at Boston Logan Airport for more than 25 years. The snowy owls' natural habitat is the Arctic tundra—a treeless stretch of open grass. The broad expanse of land around airport runways resembles tundra and becomes winter hunting grounds for owls. Owls find meadow voles and rats to be fine fare at airports. Smith watched a snowy owl pick off airport mallards one by one. He thought that when there was only one duck left in the flock, the quacker would have considered relocating. It did not and the owl had another meal.

Birding Buses

I spent the night at the home of good friends—John and Susan Kroll of Long Prairie, Minnesota. Over a delicious breakfast of oatmeal smothered in cream and maple syrup, the discussion moved to buses. The three of us have spent time on many buses used at birding festivals. Those buses break down occasionally. I have been on buses that have become stuck, gone into ditches, had transmissions go out, and had engines fail. John and Susan were on a bus that became disabled. The passengers grabbed their binoculars and went birding on foot. That's making the best of a bird situation.

Waterfowl

The melted snow had created a vernal pond in a tilled farm field. I saw good-sized flocks of ducks fly into the temporary wetland. I set up a scope in my office and my bride and I watched the waterfowl with a mixture of wonder and awe. I watched northern shovelers waddle across the muddy water that would be transformed into a cornfield. Northern pintail, mallards, and American wigeons joined them.

The ducks might not have known that the water would be leaving. They might not have cared. Too much water is a problem for so many people, but I couldn't help but enjoy its brief abundance. I knew that the ducks and the water would both leave. I hoped they would take their time.

Swan Song

Pastor Cherie Daniel called my wife and reported many swans not far from our home. Shortly thereafter, I drove into our garage. Upon my arrival home, I promptly left again—this time, taking my wife with me. I drove north, pulled up behind Cherie's car, and parked. Cherie and Vernell Miller greeted us. I employed my binoculars and scanned the wet farm fields. Geese, ducks, and hundreds of tundra swans were presented in easily digestible bursts of birding. All the waterfowl were incredibly lovely, but there is something special about swans. The big white birds brought a degree of deliciousness to my already superb day. I listened to the sounds of the swans (once called "whistling swans"), Canada and greater white-fronted geese, mallards (it's the female that quacks), and the squeaky-toy call of the American wigeons (baldpates). I love the noise of birds. It keeps my ears on their toes.

Chimney Swifts Love a Good Chimney

I was sitting on the sidewalk across the street from a commercial enterprise. I was watching a smokestack at dusk—odd behavior even for an odd fellow like me. I was waiting for chimney swifts to go to roost. Appearing to be "flying cigars," the swifts twittered overhead as they captured flying insects. Swifts fly constantly except when at the nest or roosting at night. The swift bathes in flight. It flutters to water, strikes the surface with its body, and shakes the water from its feathers in flight. The chimney swift's nest is a half-saucer of small twigs held together with saliva and glued with saliva to the inside wall of a chimney.

As I kept an eagle eye out for swifts above the smoke-stack, a man walked near. He asked me what I was doing. I told him. He gave me a sympathetic smile and said, "Well, good luck with that," before walking away, shaking his head.

I watched 150 chimney swifts zoom into that smoke-stack. I had good luck with that.

Boat Swallows

I was speaking on a tour boat on a lovely lake. As we left the dock, barn swallows had a collective cow. I quickly discovered the reason for the swallows' distress. Two young barn swallows, newly fledged, were stowaways. The parents followed the boat for some distance before giving up and heading back to shore. The juvenile swallows perched silently upon a boat's speaker and gazed at their shipmates. When the short tour ended and the boat returned to the dock, it was greeted by loud and happy sounds of not only the parent swallows but also of their friends and neighbors. The baby swallows twittered gleefully in response.

Binocular Lust

I think binoculars should have a better name. Something like "lookers" or "gawkers." Binoculars by any other name would see as sweet.

My first binoculars weren't even binoculars. They were Grandma Cook's ancient opera glasses. Incredible as it sounds, they were able to make things appear to be as close as they actually were. I don't think Grandma ever attended the opera, but she listened to it regularly on the radio. Maybe she used the opera glasses to watch the radio. I was OK birding with opera glasses. They had a dandy handle, and I was set in case I received an invitation to a royal wedding. The opera glasses worked, but I poked myself in the eye with the handle while trying to see a cerulean warbler in the treetops.

I wanted something better than opera glasses for admiring things from a distance. I couldn't find any optics in a box of Cracker Jacks, so I considered X-ray Specs. I'd seen an ad in the funny books (comic books) that read, "Scientific optical principle really works. Imagine—you put on the 'X-ray' Specs and hold your hands in front of you. You seem to be able to look right through the flesh and see the bones underneath. Look at your friend. Is that really his body you 'see' under his clothes? Loads of laughs and fun at parties. Send only $1 plus 25 cents shipping charges. Money Back Guarantee. Honor House Products Corp. Lynbrook, New York."

I walked miles of bean rows pulling countless weeds to raise the money to buy those X-ray Specs. Those were in the dark days before child-labor or minimum-wage laws were enforced. I thought I'd be able to see birds hidden behind leaves with X-ray Specs, but later I couldn't even see why I bought the Specs.

It's human nature to want something better than what we have. I like ants on a log. That's what I call peanut butter smeared onto a stalk of celery and topped with raisins. It's unfailingly good, but there are always bigger and sweeter raisins. There will always be better and sweeter binoculars.

I was birding a prairie with a flock of folks in North Dakota. The birds were cooperative, so a skirmish line of spotting scopes was set up. I stepped back to talk to the trip leader, Ron Martin. He greeted me with "Acme seems to be doing well."

Acme isn't the real name of a binoculars company. Wile E. Coyote and his rocket-powered binoculars weren't birding with us. Acme was doing well without him. Most everyone in the group had Acme binoculars or spotting scopes. If they didn't, they wore Acme hats. I discerned only two birders lacking an Acme product—Ron Martin and me.

Later, on the same trip, I heard the sound Acme binoculars make when accidentally dropped on the pavement in a parking lot. It's "Aaaaarrrrrgggghhhh!" Only much louder.

Equipping a birding hick like me with such fine binoculars as Acme might be akin to putting perfume on a hog. I once left my binoculars on the seat of my parked car. Someone broke a window of the vehicle and placed nicer binoculars next to mine.

Would I like better binoculars? Of course. It's natural to want to enhance our abilities to see and identify birds. We don't want to leave anything in the bag. Good binoculars make everything we see an optical illusion—in a good way. We hope that better binoculars snap our lives into focus.

I was at Hawk Ridge in Duluth and hanging out by Frank Nicoletti, an amazing hawk counter.

"Cooper's hawk straight out. Female," Frank stated.

I couldn't even see a bird. I looked at the binoculars used by the raptor recorder extraordinaire. I thought they would have been magical. Instead, they were ancient and battered. They worked for Frank.

I like binoculars that don't show the dirt. Bill Thompson, III, is a master at cleaning binoculars. He's such a great guy that he offers this free service to birders, and the binoculars come back cleaner than when they'd left the factory. Bill cleans optics with such gusto that he could make a living at it. I like something spilled on my binoculars. If there is a little ketchup on a lens, it means that I'll see something. A strategically placed drop of mustard can make a yellow-headed blackbird out of a grackle.

Sometimes the nicest thing about not being able to afford expensive binoculars is not being able to afford expensive binoculars. My favorite binoculars were given to me by my mother. She bought them on sale at Monkey Wards. They weren't expensive in a monetary measure, but in sentimental value they were priceless. I used them for years until they were stolen. They're my dream binoculars. I dream of getting them back.

It's not easy finding dream binoculars. It's like reaching barehanded into a beehive and trying to grab the queen. Binoculars need to fit you and be your friend. Name them. They won't come when you call, but you'll have a name to use when you talk to them. And you will talk to them. Don't worry what people will think. They'll assume your binoculars have a built-in cell phone.

Binoculars should knock your socks off when you look through them. Losing socks that way can be distracting, but you'll get used to it.

There are many things to be said for buying expensive binoculars. You've heard them from other birders or read them in this magazine's expert reviews. One thing that isn't often mentioned is that if you buy expensive binoculars, you might be more inclined to use them. Your investment will demand it. You'll become more likely to leave the house without pants than without binoculars. That might be a good thing, depending on how you look without pants and how tolerant the local police are. If the binoculars encourage you to go birding, they are worth it. Birding is like flossing. It's more effective if you do it every day.

I'll continue to drool over new binoculars. I'll hope to win a binoculars-coveting contest because I want it more.

What I write won't stop anyone from buying new binoculars. It won't even stop me. Buying binoculars is good for the economy and good for birding. Buy binoculars studded with diamonds or covered in chrome if you want. I think everyone should buy swell binoculars and give the old ones to a worthy cause or to another birder. Give them to a youngster interested in birds.

A friend told me of his uncle's death. I knew the uncle only slightly but liked what I knew of him.

"What did he die of?" I asked.

"Nothing," my friend replied. "He just wore out."

That would be a good end for binoculars.

Chapter 5:
Ask Al

The Call of the Wild

I met the couple from Dayton, Ohio. Her name was Mary, she was undergoing chemo, and it had been hard on her. Mary had managed to maintain a great smile and a bubbly personality.

A small flock of Canada geese flew overhead as we visited.

Mary looked up at the big birds and said, "Oh, please honk. Please honk."

She looked and listened as if it might have been her last opportunity to hear geese. I silently hoped that it would not be. I yearned to hear the geese call.

The geese honked. Mary glowed.

I'd never been so happy to hear the honking of geese.

Grabbing Grackles

It was at breakfast when he told me his story.

He has grackles that nest in his yard.

He informed me that he had been watching as two of the birds, which he refers to as blackbirds, built nests in adjacent trees.

He related to me that he had been watching one bird steal material from the other's nest.

Avian larceny.

He asked me if this was common.

I told him that it does happen.

He replied, "Why, they're no better than humans."

The Chickadee Hunter

The hunter told me that he was situated in a deer stand, waiting for that trophy buck of his dreams to venture into his sights.

A tiny chickadee flew in and landed on the barrel of his gun.

The chickadee peered at the hunter through tiny black eyes.

The hunter smiled at the chickadee.

The hunter didn't even catch a fleeting glimpse of a buck that day.

The hunter said he didn't mind.

From the Mailbag

Dear Al,

I have three brothers. One is a birder and the other two are in prison for the rest of their lives. My mother is in an insane asylum. My father is a drug dealer. My sister is a kleptomaniac.

Recently, I met a girl who just graduated from reform school. She was there because she couldn't stop stealing cars. I want to marry this car thief.

My problem is this: If I marry this girl, should I tell her about my brother who is the birder?

Sincerely, Worried in Warroad.

A Black-Winged Redbird

A caller said she had seen a beautiful bird and wondered if it could have been a scarlet tanager.

I asked her what she had said when she first saw the bird.

She replied that she had said, "Wow!"

I said, "Then it was a scarlet tanager."

It's a Nutty World

Lee Smith of Richfield, Minnesota, a former Navy fireman, told me that he had a tame squirrel that he befriended by feeding peanuts to it on a daily basis. One day, the mailman, also a friend of Lee's, stopped with the mail. As he handed the mail to Lee, Lee tossed a couple of peanuts into the mailman's bag. The squirrel crawled into the mailbag in pursuit of the goobers. The mailman's routine day suddenly became one filled with much befuddlement, interlaced with panicked dancing. Lee had some explaining to do.

Chipmunks and Crisco

A friend related a story of an interesting encounter she had with nature.

She and her husband put up a number of birdhouses in their yard in the hopes of enticing house wrens to take up residence. Looking out her window one day, she noticed a house sparrow fluttering in front of one of the houses. She didn't think much about it at the time. Later, she noticed that the bird was still fluttering about at the wren house. This seemed odd. She decided to investigate the sparrow's actions. She discovered that the sparrow, in an attempt to get inside the wren house, had gotten its head stuck in the entrance hole and was unable to free itself. Some folks would not be very concerned about the plight of a house sparrow. Many people consider them an avian gang member of the worst kind. Most people would probably clear the entrance hole by dispatching the intruding sparrow in a humane way, but not my friend. Her heart won't allow her to do such things. Her heart is big enough to have room for even the lowly sparrow. She tried to wriggle the brown bird out of the confining hole, but the wooden house refused to loosen its headlock. She thought fast and retreated to her kitchen. She came back out with a can of Crisco. She greased up the head feathers of the struggling sparrow. After a bit of feather dressing was applied, the sparrow's head popped free. She released the sparrow in her yard. The last she saw of it, the bird was busy preening and trying to degrease itself. I suspect it was attempting to figure out what in the world had just happened to it. This is probably how avian alien abduction stories start.

This story reminded me of a day at my house, the Batt Cave, some years ago.

I came home in the evening after playing in a softball game. Our faithful canine companion—Gus—was on the deck, staring into the house through the patio door. I thought it a little strange, but then he was an extremely strange dog. I figured he just wanted into the house.

I walked into our abode. I stopped in the kitchen to find myself some cranberry juice to quench my thirst. After pouring a glass of the stuff, I walked into the living room to see what had gone on during my absence.

I could not help but notice something more than a little out of the ordinary on the floor of that room. There was a long line of peanuts, running single-file from the patio door (the very same one that Gus was looking into) to the sofa. This is where I encountered my wife, The Queen B. She had a sheepish look on her face. I looked down at the peanuts again and she began to explain their presence.

It seems that she had opened the door to let Gus out onto the deck for one of his 272 daily forays there. Gus had a "Things to do list" that required him to go in and out as often as possible. As he exited the house, he surprised a chipmunk that had been lounging on the deck. The chippy let out a frightened "Cheep!" and with all of its tail hairs standing on end, the tiny rodent bolted to what it thought was safety. In other words, it ran the opposite way that Gus was moving. The chipmunk ran inside the house through the still open patio door. This action did not go unnoticed by Gus. He turned quickly and lunged for the chipmunk. The Queen B. worried about the safety of the friendly chipmunk, slammed the glass door shut just in time to allow Gus to smash his face against it. The chipmunk, intent on survival, made a beeline for the sofa and refused to come out from under it despite my wife's threats and pleadings.

So The Queen B concocted a plan to lure the chipmunk out from under the couch by tempting it with a line of 239 peanuts. She thought that this would be a bonanza for a peanut-deprived chipmunk and would be an offer it could not refuse.

She put the peanuts in place as Gus looked on in astonishment.

That was where I came in. Her plan had failed.

Plan B was immediately put into action.

Gus was moved to the porch. The patio door was opened wide. The sofa was moved and my wife and I chased the poor chipmunk around the house until it bounded out the door to freedom. Where, we hoped, it would lead a happy and productive life.

I worry that the next time this happens—and it will—that my lovely bride will dispense with the peanut routine and will try putting Crisco on the chipmunk's head in order to get him out.

It's just a matter of time.

Talon a Tale

A friend of mine works in raptor rehabilitation in Alaska. Years ago, a bald eagle was placed in his care. The bird had an injured wing. The veterinarian claimed that its prognosis was good. The bird was expected to recover fully and be released back into the wild one day. There was one big "if."

The bald eagle, like any good athlete, should recover, but it would take a lot of work to strengthen the recovering wing.

My friend put the bird on a short tether and every morning he would run with eagle. He'd run about 200 yards while the eagle flapped above him.

This running was done in a residential area.

One day, a police car showed up outside my friend's house.

My friend walked out and asked the policemen if there was a problem.

The police officer told him that one of his neighbors had reported an eagle flying down, grabbing a man, and attempting to fly off with him.

At Least It's Not Illegal

A friend of mine, Kerry Seifert, told me a delightful story while we were both in Haines, Alaska, looking at bald eagles.

Schoolchildren were looking at the many eagles there.

Bald eagles do not get the white heads and white tails until they are 4 to 6 years old.

As the children looked at an immature, brown-colored eagle, one asked, "Is that a grown-up eagle?"

"No," came the reply from another child. "That's an amateur eagle."

His Mother Wanted Him to Meet a Nice Gull

The caller shared a cautionary tale with me.

He was calling from his combine.

A cell phone user in the middle of a large farm field.

A gull had flown into the side of the cab of the combine.

The caller picked the gull up. He declared it deceased, decided to take it home and placed it in the cab of his combine. He intended to use a field guide in his home to identify the species of the gull after he had finished harvesting the field.

When he called me, a miracle had occurred.

The gull had risen from the dead like Lazarus and was flapping around the inside of the cab of the combine.

The caller asked me what he should do.

I was so pleased to be able to give him a useful answer.

I advised him to open the door of the cab.

They'd Do the Same for Me

The tree had fallen in a heavy wind.

The owner of the tree called me because he had discovered that the tree housed a nest cavity occupied by a family of American kestrels.

There were five young kestrels—once known as "sparrow hawks"—in the nest.

I arrived at the caller's farm equipped with a bluebird nest box and good intentions. I had made the hole of the bluebird box big enough to fit a kestrel. I introduced myself to the homeless immature kestrels.

The tiny raptors flopped over onto their backs and flashed their talons in my direction.

I carefully placed each of the young falcons into the nest box.

I picked a tall tree similar to the fallen one in which to place the bluebird box.

The owner of the farm provided a rickety ladder that had been well used before the turn of the century.

I climbed the weary rungs of that ladder and attached

the bluebird box to the tree.

The view from my perch was breathtaking. The shaking ladder took my breath away.

I came back down the ladder and kissed terra firma.

By the time my feet had touched ground, the mother bird was looking in the hole of the nest box.

I was so happy to be on the ground, but I was even happier to see that the nestlings would be well taken care of.

A Loonatic

The caller asked me to come to the shopping mall.

I thanked him for the invitation but explained that I wasn't much of a shopper.

The caller wanted me to pick up a loon at the mall.

Pick up a loon? Who was selling loons at the mall? That wouldn't be legal.

The caller explained that there was a loon in the mall parking lot.

As the skunk said when the wind changed, "It all comes back to me now." Loons were in migration and the weather had been rainy. The loon had mistaken the wet parking lot for a lake. Come on, who hasn't done that? It landed on the pavement and became stranded, as loons are unable to take flight from land. I thanked the caller and prepared for a rescue mission.

I grabbed Towhee's blankie. Yes, my dog had a blankie. There's nothing wrong with that. I'll bet Lassie had a blankie. We all have issues, and if a blankie helps, it's a good thing. It was the biggest blanket in the house, and I planned to use it to capture the loon. Towhee gave me that sad-eyed look that said "Why me?" She didn't like me swiping her blankie. It had been used in other rescue missions and it meant that her blankie would be washed and hung on a line. That left Towhee without a blankie. A sad state.

I threw the blanket in my car and headed to the mall. My thoughts went to a pelican that I'd rescued from the ice of a lake the previous winter. A police officer had called and told me of a pelican with an injured wing. I suspected the bird had collided with a utility wire. The officer stood on land as I walked on ice as thin as a supermodel. I have 100 billion brain cells (give or take a few billion), but none of them were working that day. As I stepped gingerly on the ice, I had a severe case of elevator stomach. I thought of Wyatt Earp's last word, which is said to have been "Suppose." My last words would have been "Suppose I'd stayed off the ice."

The pelican was as easy to grab as a shadow, but I was able to throw Towhee's blanket over the bird and take it to a wildlife rehabilitation center. The good folks there would do all the heavy lifting. The pelican displayed a feisty attitude. It had the world-class bad breath of someone who gargled regularly with cod liver oil. It punched me so hard with its good wing that my shoelaces came untied.

As I drove toward the loon, my thoughts traveled to the aftermath of a storm years ago. A tornado had taken down many trees and a neighbor phoned to tell me that a nest of American kestrels was at peril in a fallen tree. My plan was to attach a flicker box high on a standing tree and place the young kestrels in the replacement tree cavity. It was a good idea except for the widow-maker of a ladder that the neighbor provided. I decided that I was an idiot whether I climbed the ladder or not, so up I went. As I placed the babies into the nest box, the parent kestrels buzzed my tower. That put even more wobble into my day. I tried not to scream like a noon whistle as I climbed up and down a ladder that should have been a scary ride at some amusement park. It had a happy ending. I hadn't stopped kissing the ground before I saw the mother kestrel flying into the nest box to check on her five nestlings.

I don't tell my long-suffering wife about these escapades until well after the statutes of limitations have expired. There is a reason that the neighbors call her "Poor Mrs. Batt."

It was a dark and stormy night as I turned into the mall parking lot. I used my turn signals. I had to. I was from out of town. Locals don't use turn signals because everyone knows where they are turning. I was behind the wheel of my Pontiac—which stands for "Poor Old Nincompoop Thinks It's A Cadillac." It carried a bumper sticker reading "Start seeing birds." It wasn't a real bumper sticker. I had used a magic marker to print the words on duct tape. It added a touch of class. I'm working on another bumper sticker that will read, "Will work for birds."

I found the loon illegally parked in a tow-away zone. It appeared unhurt. I looked at its daggerlike bill that made thin ice and rickety ladders appealing. I had to help the loon. I had no choice. It's our state bird here in Minnesota. If I didn't help it, who would? I didn't know how to contact Mark Trail, Jack Hanna, or Tarzan. The Crocodile Hunter was no longer available. Guilt is a powerful motivator. I told myself that my rescue wouldn't be hairy enough to make a toupee for a grape.

I slogged along slowly in the downpour. The loon scooted awkwardly, and after a brief chase I was able to corral it in a blanket. I did it without being stabbed—a definite bonus. Wet people watched as if the loon and I were in a parade.

I carried the struggling bird wrapped in a blanket to my car. It was like a Far Side cartoon without a clever caption. I looked like a deranged but dedicated deliveryman, but

I'm sure people were calling the police to report a possible kidnapping.

I got into the car. Everything smelled like a wet dog. Towhee would have been proud.

I took the loon to a large lake and released it. It disappeared quickly into the watery darkness. I wished it well.

I drove home basking in the glow of a good deed done.

At home, I hung Towhee's blankie on the clothesline. It was still raining, but the blanket couldn't have gotten any wetter. The sun would come out tomorrow.

I smiled.

I think Brad Pitt should play me in the movie.

Outhouse Ornithology

Ben told me that he had grown up near Detroit Lakes. His family did not have indoor plumbing. They had an outhouse instead. One night, nature called long after darkness had fallen. A very young Ben trudged to the little house out back. Ben was about to enter the structure when a large owl flew out of the outhouse. Ben fell to the ground in surprise. Ben said the incident disturbed him so that he had to walk to the neighbors to use their outhouse. He added that he had no trouble going.

Watching Birds

The farmer told me that he once ran his tractor through his neighbor's fence because he was distracted while watching turkey vultures in flight.

In *Mending Wall*, Robert Frost told us that good fences make for good neighbors.

Experience tells us that watching birds can make for poor fences.

Oriole or Oreo?

A friend named Bill Bryson of Alden, Minnesota was at a checkout in a supermarket. He was buying grape jelly—a lot of grape jelly. Bill uses it to feed to the orioles in his yard. As the cashier rang up Bill's purchases, she commented on the amount of grape jelly. Bill replied that he used it for his orioles. The busy cashier responded, "Oh, I've never tried it on a cookie."

One-Sided Bird Conversations

A friend named Tom Bell from St. Paul is an avid birder. He often walks down a trail with his wife Elizabeth. They love to listen to the birds. Tom said that it was strange that all the birds he heard were on one side of the trail, while his wife was hearing birds on both sides of the trail. Tom has a hearing aid now and joyfully listens to the birds singing on both sides of the trail.

Birding Techniques of the Poor and Fatuous

Seymour Berdz tells me that he has learned to walk backwards when approaching birds. That way, he doesn't see them when they fly away.

Squirrels versus Feeders

Seymour Berdz tells me that he likes it when squirrels have chewed up his bird feeders because then he doesn't have to worry about squirrels chewing up his bird feeders.

Ask Al

Readers ask splendid questions.

"Why do three-toed woodpeckers have three toes?" They need the middle toe to separate the other two.

"Do barn swallows really eat barns?" No, they just peck

the grain out of the wood.

"How can I tell if a Canada goose is a male or a female?" Feed them corn. If he eats it, it's a gander. If she eats it, it's a female.

"Why do geese honk while flying in a flock?" They are asking, "Are we there yet?"

"How can I tell if an immature bald eagle is a male or a female?" My wife says that if it is immature, it's a male.

"What are squirrels up to?" Something.

"What did Columbus see flying near his ships that convinced him that he was approaching land?" A paper airplane.

When Food Flies

A friend tossed a bit of food to the mallards in a channel. One female, either shy or bullied, remained distant from the rest of the flock, which was in a feeding frenzy that would have made sharks jealous. The friend threw a hunk of food toward that hen in the hopes that she would not go hungry. It was a perfect pitch. The foodstuff hit the duck on the top of her head. She quickly retrieved the chow and was gobbling it down when a fish came up from below in a tardy attempt to grab the bait. It frightened the duck. She swallowed the food but remained nervously apart from the flock.

Squirrel 1, Man 0

Ron Evenson of Houston, Minnesota, told me that his father watched a squirrel jump over a railing and feast at a feeder meant for birds. Ron's father didn't move the feeder 10 feet away as most people would do. No, his plan was more diabolical. He moved the feeder three inches each day. This caused the squirrel to misjudge leaps and nearly miss being able to climb onto the feeder. One day, the squirrel missed. Ron's father took this as a victory. You could imagine his dismay when he looked out later to see the squirrel happily chowing down on the feeder. Ron's father became so upset with the persistent squirrel that he ran outside to chase the squirrel away. The squirrel watched as a single misstep left Ron's father with a broken leg.

Itchy Richie

The legend lives on, from Oscar on down, of the big bird they called Itchy Richie.

The circus was in town.

When he was a boy, Oscar had friends who wanted to run off and join the circus. Not Oscar. He had never been to the circus.

He read the newspaper account of the circus. It said that an ostrich named Itchy Richie was part of the spectacle. The story said that the ostrich was so large that a man could ride on its back.

"Imagine that," said Oscar to himself.

He wanted to see an ostrich. He'd seen photographs of ostriches in *National Geographic*. He'd subscribed to that magazine for so long that Oscar had seen nearly everything. The first time he saw a picture of an ostrich, he'd put seeing a live one on his bucket list. That was before there were bucket lists. Seeing an ostrich became a goal.

It would have been wonderful (maybe even twoderful) to see an ostrich but Oscar had no time to go gallivanting off to a circus. He had dirt to scratch and eggs to lay. Oscar kept chickens, and the chicken chores kept Oscar busy. Who would gather the eggs and feed the hens if Oscar went to the circus? Still, it would have been nice to see an ostrich. He'd buy an ostrich feeder if there were no perches necessary. That thought made Oscar chuckle.

Oscar sighed and turned the newspaper page. There was another story about the circus. In this article, it said that the ostrich that Oscar longed to see had escaped. Just as it was the dream of some of Oscar's boyhood friends to run off and join a circus, it might have been Itchy Richie's dream to run off and join a farm. The circus owner wanted to hear from anyone seeing the fugitive.

"Where does an ostrich hide?" Oscar wondered.

Oscar answered his own question. An ostrich didn't bury its head in the sand, but a bird big enough to guard a prison and eat a Chihuahua whole could hide anywhere it wanted. He wondered how the bird found feathers in its size.

Oscar figured that seeing an ostrich just wasn't in the cards for him. He put down the newspaper. It was time to gather eggs. He moved through the henhouse and grabbed every egg. He checked each nest twice to make sure he didn't miss an egg. He washed the eggs and placed them into crates meant to hold eggs. He slid the crates carefully into the box of his pickup truck—a truck that he'd purchased with the profits from egg sales. He climbed into the cab and started the truck. He headed down the driveway and turned onto a township road. He was driving to town to sell the hen fruit.

The road was all business but Oscar was bothered. His cows were contented but Oscar was not. Oscar didn't want much. Removing stones from a field rocked his world, but he had really wanted to see that ostrich.

Oscar wasn't driving fast. The road had bumps and he was hauling fragile cargo. He was watching the road but thinking about ostriches. A daydreaming filmstrip was running through his mind. It showed the ostrich photos he'd seen in *National Geographic*.

The filmstrip ended prematurely as it always did in

school. The film would break and the projector made that *fwut, fwut, fwut* sound. This time it was because something was coming down the road right at Oscar and his pristine pickup. Oscar sensed that whatever it was, it wasn't motorized. It moved as though it were running.

As it neared, Oscar was amazed to see that it was an ostrich. It ran straight toward his truck as though it had no intention of veering. The ostrich was playing a game of chicken with Oscar. That gave Oscar a geranium in his cranium.

Oscar didn't want to run over the only living ostrich he'd ever seen, and he didn't want to be run over by the only living ostrich he'd ever seen. Oscar swerved. He swerved too much. A tire caught the edge of the road and the truck went into the ditch. The result was a dented fender, a smashed headlight, and three eggs remaining unbroken. The yolk was on Oscar's truck as Itchy Richie the ostrich hoofed his way to the horizon.

The sheriff arrived on the scene and asked for details.

All Oscar could say was, "At least I got to see an ostrich."

Stamping the Robin

Marion Seber of Peoria, Illinois, told me that when she sees the first robin of the spring, she licks the thumb of her right hand and presses it into the palm of her left hand. This is called "stamping the robin." It assures good luck during the upcoming year, but it has to be done after the first (and only the first) robin is spotted.

Wisdom

Stan Fitz of Rockford, Iowa, was interested in gathering some wild mushrooms.

His daughter told him that he should save a piece from

every mushroom that he found and consumed. She added that the doctor would likely need to see it.

Overheard at the Hardware Store

"Do you think a rabbit could get through the holes in this fence?"

"It would have to be plenty scared."

A LIFE GONE TO THE BIRDS

Chapter 6:
Natural Wisdom

I've Been Reading

I just read Norman Melville's (Herman's cousin) wonderful book, *Moby Dickcissel*. It's an allegory about a man's quest for his dream bird.

Migration

There was a time when Canada geese were really Canada geese.

No, they didn't say "eh" a lot or carry hockey sticks. They were Canada geese because they didn't spend the summer with me. They went farther north to breed.

To the geese, I lived in flyover land. They migrated over my southern Minnesota farm located somewhere in what is known as the Gallbladder of the World. They likely didn't know or care that Hartland, Minnesota is the honeymoon capital of northern Freeborn County.

I was a hard working (my opinion and not based upon fact) farm boy during a dark period of time before child labor laws were enforced.

I watched the geese as they honk-a-lonked overhead. They weren't just geese to me. They were dreams filled with wonder and mystery. I wanted to go where they were going. I wanted to be where they had been. I wanted to see what they had seen. They were frequent fliers and I was a stay-putter. It seemed unfair. The birds could fly. I could drive a farm tractor. Not many people travel far by a John Deere. I had heard of nowhere and I was afraid that was where I lived.

I expected to see travel stickers affixed to the wings of the geese indicating the places they had been.

The geese dragged my thoughts and my hopes of travel with them.

At night, I sat on the steps of our old farmhouse. I listened to the chirps of migrating songbirds leaving me behind.

I am sure that I tried flapping my arms in the hopes of being that one mutant boy who was capable of flying. Gravity is not one to let even a small boy with big dreams off the hook. I was bound to be earthbound.

Once upon a time, my ancestors watched night sky geese fly across the face of a full moon and assumed that the birds wintered on the moon. That's why they didn't see the birds in the winter. Not many of my ancestors were the class valedictorians.

The birds didn't correct them. As vocal as they are, birds can be close-beaked about things. You can't blame them. They have been trying to tell humans things for centuries with limited success.

Birds migrate because they take meetings. Migration is how they get from where they are to where they need to be. They fly because it is too far to walk.

I hope they enjoy their flights, but I suspect that migration is a headache for birds. A migration headache. The good news for birds is that they are able to avoid airport security.

Birds need to hustle. They are a family in which both parents work at demanding jobs. They put in long hours while building a house and feeding hungry mouths.

As a comedian is famed for saying, they "get 'er done."

Those that migrate must do it twice a year in good and bad weather. They encounter storm winds, rain, snow, hail, and the gloom of night. They are like mail carriers only they have feathers and carry no mail. Other than those minor differences, they are just like mail carriers. The mail must go through and so must the birds. While traveling, birds need to avoid predators, find food, find shelter, and interest a mate. Anyone who has ever been part of a family taking a car trip across the country knows how difficult it is to accomplish those things.

Birds have no Weather Channel, GPS, security system, cellphones, or the availability of computer dating. They cannot call ahead for reservations at a nice hotel with a pool and a good restaurant.

They make it—at least enough of them make it to keep the migration going for a return trip.

I watched those geese with envy. They, as much as anything, gave me wanderlust.

I watched those geese until they had winged their way out of my sight. They may have been out of my view, but they were not out of my mind.

I am a frequent flier today, but I still watch the geese fly overhead.

Birds are my travel agents.

Birds and Beatles

I read somewhere that Paul McCartney liked birds so much as a boy that he considered becoming an ornithologist. Just think, he could have become a famous bird geek, a name on the tip of everyone's tongue, instead of a forgotten musician with a little known group called The Beatles.

Bird Meteorologists

"Hear the rain crow calling?" my father asked without really asking.

I pretended I didn't hear either my father or the cuckoo.

"It will be raining soon," Dad said. "We'd better hurry the haying."

The only thing worse than more work was more work at a rush. Dad knew it was going to rain because a little bird told him. The cuckoo never lied. It always rained—eventually.

In the fall, when Dad spotted the first junco (snowbird) on our farm, he told us all that it would be six weeks until the first trackable snow. He marked the date on the calendar. If the snow fell near the predicted date, Dad would marvel aloud at the amazing prophet a snowbird was. If the date wasn't close, the failed feathered seer was not mentioned.

Sometimes the juncos were right. Sometimes the weatherman on TV is right.

The most popular forecaster in nature is the woolly bear caterpillar (woolly worm). Its coloration is supposed to predict the winter. The wider its black bands, the harsher the winter would be. The wider the brown band, the milder the upcoming winter. The woolly bear is not our only natural forecaster. Birds have long provided weather forecasts for humans. The Bible says in the Book of Job, "Just ask the animals and they will teach you. Ask the birds of the sky and they will tell you."

Here are some of the sayings about avian meteorologists:
- Birds in general
  - Birds fly lower before a storm.
  - A busy birdfeeder means bad weather is coming.
  - Birds singing in the rain means the rain will stop.
  - Birds eat more just before a storm.

- —When birds stop singing and trees start swinging, a storm is on its way.
- —When birds eat a lot and then disappear, a terrible storm is very near.
- —Birds flying low, expect rain and a blow.
- —Birds flying high; the weather will be dry. Birds flying near the ground; soon you'll hear the thunder's sound.
- —If your birds are quiet, expect the thunder to boom.
- —Birds look windward so their feathers stay inward.
- —Never trust a July sky if the birds soar high.
- —An early nest is a dry spring.
- Crows
  - —Crow on the fence, rain will go hence. Crow on the ground, rain will come down.
  - —If a crow hollers in the morning, expect rain by night.
  - —Crows flying crazily indicates a storm on the way.
  - —If crows fly in pairs, expect fine weather. A crow flying alone is a sign of foul weather.
  - —When crows call, weather shifts.
- Owls
  - — A hooting owl says that the weather will be foul.
  - — Hear an owl hoot? A storm is coming.
  - — An owl hooting in the daytime means a stormy night.
- Swallows
  - — If swallows circle and call, they speak of rain.
  - — If they skim along the ground, rain is coming. But if they fly high and chirp, it will be fair.
  - — Swallows fly high; clear blue sky. Swallows fly low; rain we will know.

- Gulls
  - Sea gull, sea gull, sitting on the sand, it's a sure sign of rain when you're on land.
  - Gulls following a farmer planting seed means the ground will be blessed with ample moisture.
- Geese
  - Wild geese, wild geese going out to sea, all fine weather it will be.
  - If the goose honks high, fair weather is nigh. If the goose honks low, foul weather.
- Robins
  - If you see a robin enter a barn, expect a heavy downpour.
  - A robin singing at dawn while facing west means a change in weather by noon.
  - Should a robin go about a hedge chirping mournfully, though the day be bright and the sky cloudless, it will rain before long. When it sings cheerfully on a topmost twig, it will soon be fair, though it might then be raining.
  - A robin in the bush means rain.
  - If the robin sings loudly from the topmost of trees, expect a storm.
  - If robins approach closer to the house than normal, expect frost soon.
- Chickens—they are birds
  - If a rooster crows after a shower, the weather will be nice and clear.
  - If a chicken has its head under its wing, it is going to rain.
  - If chickens roost early, a storm is coming.
  - If a rooster crows at night, there will be rain by morning.

- A rooster crowing at night indicates bad weather is on the way.
- If a rooster crows on the nest, he will have wet feet in the morning.
• Peafowl
    - When the peacock calls, it will rain.
    - When the peacock's distant voice you hear, are you in need of rain? Rejoice, it's here.
• And the others
    - If pigeons congregate on the ridge of a house roof, it foretells a storm of rain.
    - When the grouse drum at night, there will be a deep fall of snow.
    - Hawks flying high means a clear sky; when they fly low, prepare for a blow.
    - If an osprey is seen near a house, it signals a coming flood.
    - When the thrush sings at sunset, a fair day follows.
    - When the quail is heard in the evening, fair weather is indicated.
    - When woodpeckers peck low on the trees, expect warm weather.
    - If waterfowl make more noise than usual, expect frost soon.
    - If ducks are riding far out on the lakes, expect calm weather.
    - The loon calls loudest before the storm.
    - Cranes aloft, the day is soft; swallows soar, good weather more.
    - The cuckoo in April, he opens his bill. The cuckoo in May, he sings the whole day.

The rain crow caused me to hustle while haying. The

bales were stacked at a rapid rate because of a bird.

Rain was important on the farm. Our livelihood depended upon it. Each year, we received either too much of it or not enough. That was not true of a Minnesota winter. At a certain point each year, we had had too much of Old Man Winter. We were ready to shed that season and move onto another.

My father brightened up each year when he saw the first bluebird. A mere flash of blue feathers caused him to smile and say, "Spring arrives on the wings of a bluebird."

It did.

Thoughts While Birding

Crows may lack the chromatic intensity of many birds, but I can't spend any time near a crow without getting the feeling that it knows things that mere humans do not.

A Robin Reveille

It was as dark as the inside of a pants pocket.

It was half past four in the morning.

I was standing outside a hotel near the airport in Louisville, Kentucky.

My mind was clouded with muddled thoughts that accompany lack of sleep. I am not a coffee drinker, so I was unable to jumpstart my cognitive processes in the most common method.

I heard the song of a robin singing in the darkness. It sang, *Cheer-up, cheerily*.

I did.

Why Do We Watch Birds?

I love watching birds.

Sometimes I wonder why—especially when I seek avian

treasures on one of those frigid days featuring winds that peel the skin from my bones.

The more I learn about birds, the more I realize how little I know about them.

Thomas Edison said that we don't know one millionth of one percent about anything. I take solace in that.

I believe that birds are a window into the appreciation of nature, but they are more than that. They are a door to the outdoors. The beauty and songs of birds draw us like Sirens into the woods, the wetlands, and the prairies. They give us cause to fall in love with nature.

I watched a group of people work together to assemble a jigsaw puzzle recently. I came to the realization that each bird I see is a piece to the puzzle that constitutes my existence.

Each bird is a possibility.

I love watching birds.

One Day She Will be a Doctor

My wife and I were along the Platte River near Kearney, Nebraska.

We were watching sandhill cranes. Watching the sandhill cranes coming into the Platte River at night and leaving their watery roost in the morning is perhaps the greatest wildlife spectacle in North America.

The famed naturalist John Burroughs was often accused of using the word "glorious" too often. I understand why he did as I watched the cranes soar overhead. The crane is famed in parts of the world for being a symbol of longevity. Countless paper cranes are folded each year in the art form origami.

We hadn't seen many of the large birds before we received a phone call from my son. He told us that our month-old granddaughter, Everly, had been airlifted from

New Ulm, Minnesota to Gillette Children's Hospital in St. Paul. Everly had pneumonia and some other respiratory problems (RSV). One small lung had become completely congested.

My wife and I cried. We sobbed out of pain and out of fear.

I looked to the sky through reddened and teary eyes. I saw a number of cranes on our journey home.

Each of them carried my prayers on its wings.

The Meeting

He told us that we had a severe nonlinear waterfowl issue.

Our looks betrayed our confusion.

He clarified his comments by saying, "We don't have all our ducks in a row."

Lessons from a Child

I was leading a group of children through a state park.

I had equipped each of them with binoculars and we were doing some serious bird looking.

An ovenbird called loud and louder.

I shared with my charges that the ovenbird was singing, *Teacher, teacher, teacher.*

One boy, who had obviously been paying attention to his surroundings, said, "It sounds to me like it's saying, *Nature, nature, nature.*"

I couldn't argue with him.

Just Wondering

If a crow had a Botox injection, would it still have crow's feet?

Noah was a Birder

Genesis 8:6-12 reads, "After forty days Noah opened the window he had made in the ark and sent out a raven, and it kept flying back and forth until the water had dried up from the earth. Then he sent out a dove to see if the water had receded from the surface of the ground. But the dove could find no place to set its feet because there was water over all the surface of the earth; so it returned to Noah in the ark. He reached out his hand and took the dove and brought it back to himself in the ark. He waited seven more days and again sent out the dove from the ark. When the dove returned to him in the evening, there in its beak was a freshly plucked olive leaf! Then Noah knew that the water had receded from the earth. He waited seven more days and sent the dove out again, but this time it did not return to him."

A Late Start

I found myself counting starlings perched on a utility wire. I didn't want to. I had to. Looking at birds is never a waste of time. A friend named Jim Danzenbaker, a field representative with Kowa, took up birding when he was only six years old. Jim says that he completely wasted the first six years of his life.

Flabbergasted

Flabbergast means to overwhelm with wonder or surprise. If you are flabbergasted, you are astonished with something. Take a good look out your window. Keep looking until you are flabbergasted by something in nature. It shouldn't take long.

Things are Looking Up for Looking Down

I was waiting for someone to pick me up at the ferry terminal in Haines, Alaska. I was looking up at the antics of magpies and ravens. A van parked near me, a man stepped out, and picked up a $20 bill from under his foot. I need to look down occasionally.

The Sunset

A sunrise brings prospects.

A sunset brings memories.

A friend once told me that I should always awaken in time to see the sunset. A sunset is a sunrise with better hours.

The lower western sky hoards the sun. The sunset brings with it a quiet that allows the voice of my thoughts to be heard. I become an apprentice to the silence. Rumi said, "There is a thread from the heart to the lips where the secret of life is woven. Words tear the thread, but in silence the secrets speak."

The hush of the evening is interrupted only by the scolding of a robin.

The sun melts into the horizon and I am left with an appreciation of the day and the promise of a tomorrow.

I soak up the beauty of the exhausted day. I watch without needing to swipe a credit card. The splendor at day's end leaves me with a profound sense of gratitude.

Buddha asked, "Which way does a flame go when it has gone out?"

I know where the flame goes. It goes right to the heart.

A Yellow Bill

"A birdie with a yellow bill, hopped upon my window sill, cocked his shining eye and said:

'Ain't you 'shamed, you sleepyhead!'"

Robert Louis Stevenson wrote those words, and he could have been describing the European starling. The dark bill that the starling sports in the winter turns yellow in the spring.

The Rabbit on the Moon

Oh, I've heard the stories about the man on the moon.

I didn't believe them for an instant.

I was raised to believe that there is a rabbit on the moon.

The next time we have a full moon, get out your binoculars or spotting scope, and have a good look at the moon. You will see the long ears and the big feet, and you will know the truth. It is a rabbit on the moon.

Rabbits can hop, but getting to the moon is a sizeable leap for a bunny. Neither the post office, UPS, nor FedEx make lunar deliveries.

You are likely wondering how a rabbit got on the moon. I am so glad you are wondering that, because I am going to tell you the true story about that rabbit on the moon.

Once upon a time, long, long ago, there was a rabbit that spent his days eating plants and hopping about the earth's surface. This rabbit had a goal in life. Everyone should have a goal. He wanted to live on the moon. Now rabbits have never been good at flying and the moon was too far away for hopping, so the rabbit needed help in making his dream come true.

The rabbit hopped around, thinking about how to make its dreams come true until he came upon a red-tailed hawk.

"Hello, Mr. Hawk," said the rabbit. "Would you be willing to fly me to the moon?"

"No," replied the hawk. "But I would be willing to eat you."

"I'm just getting estimates. Let me get back to you on that," said the rabbit and quickly hopped down the road.

Soon the rabbit came upon a bald eagle.

"Hello, Mr. Eagle," said the rabbit. "Would you be willing to fly me to the moon?"

"Sure," said the eagle. "but it's a mighty long trip to the moon. Why I'll bet it's at least 50 or 60 miles. I might get hungry half the way there and if I did, I'd have to eat you."

"Thanks," said the rabbit. "That's the best deal that I've found so far, but I'm going to do a little more checking around."

Down the road the rabbit hopped until he came upon a sandhill crane. The crane was a plain gray bird with short legs.

"Hello, Mr. Crane," said the rabbit. "Would you fly me to the moon?"

"I'd be happy to," said the crane. "Grab my legs and away we'll go."

The rabbit clutched the crane's legs and away they went. The eagle was right; it was a very long flight—even longer than 50 or 60 miles. A small weight carried for a long time becomes heavy. The weight of the rabbit combined with the length of the flight caused the crane's legs to be stretched longer and longer.

Finally, the two landed on the moon. The rabbit was so happy he was hoppy. He jumped for joy and patted the crane on the top of the bird's head. The rabbit had held on so tightly to the crane's legs that he had gotten blisters on his paws. The blisters had popped and begun to bleed. When the rabbit touched the top of the crane's head, it left a red spot there.

From that day on, sandhill cranes have had long legs and a red crown.

And from that day on, there has been a rabbit on the moon.

You don't have to take my word for it. Take a look for yourself.

A Flock

A flock of birds can be identified by collective nouns such as a scold of jays, a murder of crows, a gaggle of geese, a murmuration of starlings, and a charm of finches.

There are other collective nouns that, although not in use, should be. Here are a few: an extinction of dodos, a gulp of swallows, a dichotomy of black-and-white warblers, a Waterloo of Bonaparte's gulls, a sorority of redheads, a ladle of dippers, a cushion of pintails, a cord of wood ducks, a grumbling of grouse, a marathon of roadrunners, a revenge of Montezuma quail, and a liturgy of vesper sparrows.

The Meadowlark

Birds are more important than we think.

Birds are more important than we can think.

Memories are fragile. That is why we should write things down. If we don't write them down, they go away. They don't always return.

I believe that and because I believe that, I ended up teaching a journaling class to a group of retired farmers.

They were wonderful people even if they didn't all want to be in the class. I told the good folks that recollections are ephemeral. It doesn't matter how old a person is. If things are worth remembering, they are worth writing down. If the classroom had been a church, the women were sitting in sinner's row—right up front because they needed to hear the sermon. The men were seated not just in the back. They were way in the back, like good Lutherans who come to church early so they would be able to sit in the rear.

As I offered exercises meant to aid in the journaling process, the women's writing hands were a blur as they inked their remembrances into notebooks. I rejoiced in that comforting sound of scribbling.

The men sat with their arms crossed. They were wearing the uniform of the retired farmer. They wore gimme caps advertising John Deere, DeKalb, or Pioneer. They sported bib overalls made by OshKosh B'gosh or Key and their feet hid in Red Wing work shoes.

They did not want to be there. They would rather have been almost anywhere else. They were there for only one reason. Each man was there because his wife told him that he was going to be there. If he wanted to go on that fishing trip with his cronies, he was going to take the journaling class with her.

I tried to encourage them by saying that once they had lived to be 25, they had more stories to tell than they'd be able to relate the rest of their lives.

The men gave me a collective "Harrumph!"

They informed me that they had no stories to tell because they never did anything worth putting down on paper. They milked cows. They didn't even go to town for church—theirs was a country place of worship.

I'd heard that before. I came with keys that I hoped would unlock their storeroom of memories. Scents and sounds are good bait to attract memories.

I suggested that they recall scents from their youth. The smell of the earth after a gentle rain. The fragrance of Play-Doh. The odor of mimeograph paper (an intoxicating bouquet). The aroma of that sweat sock slathered in Vicks VapoRub, wrapped about our necks, and safety-pinned into place near our jugular vein when a cold hit us.

I mentioned sounds. A father calling cows home with a repeated, "Come boss." A mother's laughter. The clatter of heavy rain or hail hitting the tin roof of a shed. That soothing sound of a treadle sewing machine at work, powered by mothers, aunts, and grandmothers.

I had these two birds with me. I squeeze them and they sing. They are not live birds. If I squeezed a live bird, it would do something other than sing and it would require a cleanup.

The birds I own are a beautiful eastern bluebird given to me by the Bluebird Recovery Program of Minnesota and a western meadowlark (the state bird of Nebraska) that the folks of the Bluebirds Across Nebraska gifted me. These are two of my favorite birds and two of my favorite organizations.

I squeezed the two stuffed birds, and rather than pooping in my hand, the two uttered exquisite bird songs recorded by the Cornell Lab of Ornithology.

The retired farmers unfolded their arms. Suddenly, those underemployed men of agriculture who claimed no remembrances of note had more stories to tell than they could write down. They told stories of haying, picnics, baseball, and fishing. Events that were accompanied by life's background music—the song of birds.

It was the song of a bird that brought back memories for these men. The bird was more than just a bird. It was a part of their lives. It was a part of those men.

Sometimes what holds people together is a shared memory. Sometimes what holds people together is a birdsong that peels away layers from forgotten moments.

A Good Evening

Butterflies, which had floated like less-than-nothing on the wind, had called it a day. I listen to the crooning of crows. They heralded the end of their day and battled the hush of sunset. The stars are waiting for the crows to quiet before they can shine. The crows are in their tree. All is right with the world.

My Faithful Canine Companion

My faithful canine companion, Towhee, died today.

She passed on while I was doing a radio show. I was pontificating over the airwaves about a green-tailed towhee and its odd presence in Mountain Lake, Minnesota, when she died.

My dog spent more time birding with me than any other living creature. She spent endless hours in my company as I searched for avian treasures. This was undoubtedly more punishment than any being should ever have been subjected to.

With binoculars in hand, I ambled towards my old Chevy pickup. Despite my head start, Towhee would easily beat me to the vehicle. With a yelp (her method of yelling "Shotgun!"), she waited thumblessly as I opened the door of the truck for her. With obvious delight and perhaps a bit of drool, she assumed her post at the passenger door window.

She was a wonderful birding partner. Towhee approached birding with a tail-wagging amazement. She was more than happy to make a meal out of an old stale doughnut. She found joy in my excitement over seeing a bird. She wasn't much for using binoculars, but would enthusiastically lick the jelly dripped from a doughnut off my optics. She listened to me without interruption, other than the occasional snoring.

She enjoyed most of the birds. She had a dislike for crows and vultures. I suspect this was based on her envy of their easy access to roadkill. She barked at the hoot of a great horned owl. Many of Towhee's conspiracy theories involved great horned owls. She believed them to be subversives of the worst kind.

I could not fill the bird feeders without Towhee. Early in her puppyhood, she had determined that I was not capable of such a task without her assistance.

Towhee was a great friend. Her love had no limits. She lived a life without expectations, criticisms, or complaints. Her presence brought me immense joy. I miss her dearly.

She gave so much and asked so little in return.

All she wanted to do was to go birding.

A Chickadee of Joy

It's a fine and pleasant day. A day meant for a leisurely walk.

It's a day to let my heart move at a pace independent of my feet.

A morning walk removes me from my everyday worries. It alters my sense of time. It gives me the opportunity to polish my brain by rubbing it against the beauty of nature. My backyard hides 100,000 mysteries.

I find a walk amongst the trees to be the perfect place to be. The sylvan delights prove that happiness has many fathers. I see a different world on these strolls. Memories come like sunlight through the branches. I find grace in my surroundings.

This was something that was instilled in me at an early age. For that I am ever grateful. Uncle Remus said in *Song of the South*, "Everybody's got a laughing place." This path that is so familiar to my feet is my laughing place.

I look up with earthbound envy at a soaring red-tailed hawk. I recall that Richard Adams in his wonderful book *Watership Down* said that rabbits identified birds as being of two kinds, hawks and not-hawks.

In the midst of being thankful that I am not a bunny, I hear a meditative whisper.

It's a marvelous world if I take the time to stop and listen to it.

The sound is the hushed murmur of a chickadee.

I watch the tiny, feathered bundle of energy and I smile.

I feel like a different person.

Is my life different because I saw a chickadee? Probably not. My life is different because of the joy that seeing a chickadee brings me. I have no control over where my heart flies. Nature gives me the opportunity to practice the art of inspired reflection. For a moment, I forget everything but this bird. This is happiness.

No miracle happens without a witness. Sometimes when I look at a chickadee, everything in my life makes sense.

We are here but for a short time. A walk in the bird-filled woods gives a sense of timelessness. We are not meant to forget such beautiful experiences as an encounter with a chickadee. They are given to us to sustain us during difficult times.

I feel more alive. That's all I can ask of a day.